Parents Want to Know

Questions for the Principal

Larry J. Stevens

ScarecrowEducation
Lanham, Maryland • Toronto • Oxford
2004

Published in the United States of America
by ScarecrowEducation
An imprint of The Rowman & Littlefield Publishing Group, Inc.
4501 Forbes Boulevard, Suite 200, Lanham, Maryland 20706
www.scarecroweducation.com

PO Box 317
Oxford
OX2 9RU, UK

British Library Cataloguing in Publication Information Available

Library of Congress Cataloging-in-Publication Data
Stevens, Larry J.
  Parents want to know : questions for the principal / Larry J. Stevens.
     p. cm.
  Includes index.
  ISBN 1-57886-170-5 (pbk. : alk. paper)
  1. Education—Parent participation. 2. School administrators—
Professional relationships. I. Title.
LB1048.5.S86 2004
371.103—dc22

                                        2004009940

©™ The paper used in this publication meets the minimum requirements of
American National Standard for Information Sciences—Permanence of
Paper for Printed Library Materials, ANSI/NISO Z39.48-1992.
Manufactured in the United States of America.

Contents

Acknowledgments

The following educators and parents contributed to the questions posed in this book. Thank you is extended for their support and assistance.

Dr. Maryann Anderson, administrator
Mrs. Shelly Brunotts, parent
Mrs. Doreen Czuba, teacher
Mr. David Dewitt, teacher
Mrs. Judith Freiwald, school secretary
Mrs. Sandra Grassel, teacher
Mrs. Paige Hanlon, teacher
Mr. Chad Krehlik, teacher
Mr. Jay Moser, teacher
Mr. Michael Porembka, teacher
Dr. Kim Quirt, school psychologist
Mrs. Nicole Rombaugh, teacher
Mrs. Cherie Rullo, teacher
Mrs. Patricia Stevens, teacher
Mrs. Linda Williams, guidance counselor

Introduction

It is essential that you ask the right questions if you are to learn about schools. To that end, this is not a book of answers; it is primarily a book of questions that can help to clarify information and assist in the understanding of many aspects related to your child's school.

In my experience of over thirty-five years in the public schools, I have found many conflicts between parents and schools are the result of misunderstandings, confusion, and a lack of information. This book, used as a reference, poses questions that can help parents avoid misunderstandings, clear up confusion, and supply the information necessary for building bridges of understanding between parents and school personnel.

What good is a book of questions? Asking the right questions helps reveal facts about the school, helps create open lines of communication, and uncovers issues in need of further discussion.

Each section in this book opens with a discussion of issues related to a specific topic. Parents will find a general background and relevant information necessary to clarify basic school issues. Following this opening discussion, subsections of questions are posed that investigate related topics. Then several specific questions are presented that parents might consider asking their principal to further clarify and delineate concerns. Finally, after each question, things to "listen/look for" are offered. While not all things to "listen/look for" may be mentioned by the principal, in many cases they serve as guidelines in gauging the depth of the school official's answers and the type of administrative responses that should be forthcoming.

Because many areas of school life overlap, some of the questions may be presented more than once. This is by design so that parents turning to a specific topic will find relevant questions related to that issue. But what should the answers be? Because of the vast differences in school districts and individual schools, specific answers cannot be provided in any one book that fit all school situations. After reviewing the questions in a specific section, considering the suggested things to "listen/look for," and inquiring at the school, the individual parent must decide if the administrator's answers provide the degree of information desired. It is the intent of this book to provide probing questions from which the appropriate answers may be more easily reached.

Principals, as instructional leaders responsible for the overall operation of their buildings, should welcome the opportunity to meet with parents and respond to their concerns and questions. Rather than feeling threatened, good principals should make every effort to point out the good things their schools are doing and openly discuss the areas still needing improvement. It is only through such honest discussions with school officials that parents begin to more fully understand, appreciate, and support school programs. Together, with principals and teachers, parents can then be more prepared to work as team members in the important job of educating children.

HOW TO USE THIS BOOK

Each section of this book is divided into four segments: a general area of concern, a short discussion of the topic, questions to ask the principal, and answers to listen and look for in his or her responses.

When parents have questions about their child's school they should do the following:

1. Refer to the relevant section of the book and read the questions related to that concern.
   (example) "Are emergency drills conducted regularly?"
2. Read the short discussion of the topic for background knowledge.
   (example) "As stated earlier . . . an actual emergency could have devastating results."

3. Scan the Questions to Consider for questions to ask the principal.
   (example) "How many emergency drills are conducted yearly?"
4. Review the "listen/look for" segment for possible answers that, hopefully, principals may include in their responses.
   (example) "monthly fire drills, tornado drill biannually, crisis drills quarterly or at least two times per year"

Parents should then schedule a meeting with their child's principal and ask pertinent questions to learn about the school.

Although usually well versed in district policies, principals may or may not immediately know all of the answers to the questions posed. The depth of the questions asked by the parent and the degree of specificity provided by the principal will help direct and focus the discussion or point out the need for additional meetings.

The questions presented are meant to stimulate serious investigation of school rules and help lead the discussion into issues often considered confusing by many parents. They are not presented to embarrass the principal or to initiate a confrontation. To the contrary, they are intended as a bridge to increase the understanding between the parent and the school. Additionally, asking probing questions identifies the parent as an individual interested in being a proactive partner in his or her child's education.

DISCLAIMER

Areas discussed in this book are general in nature because every school district and school building has specific policies, rules, and operating procedures unique to that school site. Further, this book is neither a legal guide nor a substitute for meetings with local school principals on educational matters and contact with police where security-related issues are concerned. The author takes no responsibility for the reader's reliance on the contents of this book. It is intended only as a guide to help parents better understand their child's school.

CHAPTER 1

The School

A school should be a pleasant place where students are exposed to learning opportunities. It should be orderly and well managed, with a caring staff excited about helping children learn. Rules should be reasonable and fairly enforced with consequences appropriate to the degree of misbehavior.

Schools should:
- have a rich, positive environment
- have organized instruction
- have qualified teachers
- have a safe and secure environment
- have reasonable rules
- have instructional leaders
- be open to parents' concerns
- reflect the community values

School should not:
- have a prison climate
- be solely responsible for student behavior
- be expected to be perfect
- ignore their problems
- disregard student rights
- be a closed system
- be unfriendly to parents

SCHOOL CLIMATE

The school climate is reflective of the school staff, the student body, and their interaction in all aspects of school life. The climate or ethos of a school permeates all aspects of the school, resulting in either a rich, motivating environment or a demoralizing, restrictive atmosphere. As such, the climate of a school can be altered to reflect calmness rather than chaos, order rather than disorder, and freedom of expression rather than dictatorial mandates.

Quality schools often seem to exude a feeling when first entered. There seems to be a dynamic in the air that visitors can often discern. The display of student work in the hallways can be an indication of the importance placed on the recognition of children's efforts. The movement of students in the hallways can demonstrate either an orderly transition or a hectic race to reach the next class. The first impression of the office staff can create perceptions of either an open, welcoming team or a self-absorbed, unfriendly group of workers.

The communities around the school or the parents of students attending the school have perceptions of the type of school environment that exists. While some individuals may have jaded opinions because of bad experiences with the school personnel, contacting several different parents can give a more balanced view. Some of the best indicators of the school environment are the comments of students that attend on a daily basis. Students are typically candid about the school, including its climate and daily routine. They will openly point out internal problems such as a lack of rapport between staff or students and the need for improved trust and respect within the building.

The impression that a school is a pleasant place for students is often a feeling rather than a tangible element. In most cases what students get out of school depends, to a large extent, on what they put into it.

Questions to Consider

How do parents know if the school is a pleasant place for their child?
Listen/look for: positive comments from children; the mood of the office staff; the positive attitude of the principal; the feeling one gets when entering the building

What recognition programs are conducted in the school?
Listen/look for: art shows; musical concerts; award assemblies; special recognition programs; special days recognizing individual students; honor rolls

Is the office staff nice to parents but harsh when dealing with children?
Listen/look for: response to and attitude toward children coming to the office; how they answer the phone; comments of a positive nature regarding work in the school; a willingness to help children

What do neighborhood children like about the school?
Listen/look for: their attitude toward teachers; their feelings about enjoying school; how involved they are in school activities; the spirit shown toward sports teams; their excitement about upcoming school events

How do teachers, custodians, and office staff say things are going?
Listen/look for: comments made between professionals; overheard complaints about school programs or rules; the response to requests from teachers and support staff

Are there smiles on the faces of students, teachers, and the principal?
Listen/look for: smiles, not only when talking to you, but when conversing among each other; a sense of humor; a genuine enjoyment of their jobs

Is the school graffiti-free?
Listen/look for: clean restrooms; exterior walls free of gang signs, spray paint, and other markings; lockers free of names and scribbling

Are classrooms well cared for and orderly?
Listen/look for: reasonably clean floors and hallways; papers and other teaching supplies arranged in an orderly fashion; chalkboards that have been cleaned; fairly neat desks and noninstructional areas

Is the Creative Work of Students Valued?

As mentioned previously, the display of student artwork, the showcasing of student projects, musical programs, and other types of student creativity are positive signs that a school is interested in promoting student recognition within the school. Typically, elementary schools are more prone to display student artwork. But secondary schools should also take pride in the efforts of their students and take steps to highlight student creative work in every area.

Take note of the classrooms to see if student papers are displayed. Are students' drawings and illustrations part of bulletin boards and used as part of ongoing lessons, or is every picture in the school a commercially prepared poster? The use of student-prepared displays as part of the teacher's lesson is an excellent sign that the school values the talents and skills of students.

Questions to Consider

Where is artwork displayed in the school?
Listen/look for: showcases in the lobby; student pictures in the office; student artwork in the hallways and classrooms; student paintings in the gym

How are student creative efforts promoted?
Listen/look for: indications that student work is appreciated; pictures of students used as signs of recognition; honor roll postings; names of students of the week or other indication of student recognition

What kind of medium does the art teacher use?
Listen/look for: the variety of medium (clay, paint, drawing, crafts, and so on) displayed in the art room; presence of a kiln; variety of student work displayed showing mixed application of oil, acrylic, water paint, ceramics, enameling, pencil, and craft projects

What musical concerts are held?
Listen/look for: advertisements of upcoming musical events (spring concert, holiday concert); notices in the local paper of band, choral, or orchestra programs

Is there a school (student) newspaper?
Listen/look for: copies of student newspapers in the office; notices posted of recent student articles

Is there a student council?
Listen/look for: pictures of student council officers; listings of student council events; names of officers in student handbooks; announcements being made by student council members

Does the School Seem Like a Prison?

Recently, schools have had to increase security measures. As a result, school doors are often locked during the school day and entrance is permitted only through the use of a buzzer system. Likewise, limitations may be in place regarding parental access to classrooms and other areas where students congregate. This is an unfortunate but necessary reality in today's schools. While the outward appearance of the school may display intensified attention to safety and security, such precautions need not be implemented in an unreasonable, restrictive, or punitive manner. Students have a right to feel safe in their school. They need to know that their school, regardless of the events in the community around them, has procedures in place to protect them.

Parents need to realize the necessity of recent security measures. They must adjust to the fact that safety can never be jeopardized for the sake of convenience. Parents and the community need to view the school as a place that is safe for children and school personnel, yet welcoming to individuals with valid reasons to visit.

Questions to Consider

Do students seem happy as they pass you in the hallways?
Listen/look for: laughing children; sounds of enjoyment; smiles on their faces; children chatting with each other in a calm, pleasant manner

What is the behavior and attitude of the children while eating lunch?
Listen/look for: children eating in an orderly, casual manner; children seated as they eat, with no excess movement; used trays being placed in the appropriate location; children asking questions of the teacher on duty in a respectful manner; a noise level that reflects children eating and quietly talking; no excessive noise and loud voices

Are students actively engaged in class activities?
Listen/look for: classroom behavior that reflects respect for the teacher; controlled movement within the classroom; appropriate excitement directed at the activity; movement in direct relationship to the specific teacher-directed activity

Are school signs and posters stated in positive, optimistic terms?
Listen/look for: signs that read "Please Walk" rather than "Don't Run," "Please Remain Quiet" rather than "No Talking," "Please Remain Seated" rather than "No Standing"

Does entrance into the school entail excessive time and unnecessary procedures?
Listen/look for: welcome signs; clearly identified entrances; visitor parking signs; clearly stated directions to the office; necessary signs to

direct visitors to public areas (gym, auditorium); uncomplicated sign-in procedures and visitor badges; maps provided or guides available to assist visitors

Is the school well lit in the evening?
Listen/look for: well-lit entrances; well-lit parking lots near the building; hallways with adequate lighting; all exterior doors unlocked from the inside and marked with emergency exit signs

Is there an active sports program?
Listen/look for: posters and pictures of school teams; spirit signs indicating the next scheduled games; signs proclaiming the esprit de corps of the school

Do students respect the school?
Listen/look for: absence of writing on restroom and exterior walls, graffiti on the walls near water fountains, spray paint on the signs near the school; limited paper and litter on the hallway floors; absence of gum in water fountains

Are the Teachers Friendly?

Everyone has memories of the school they attended. Most parents had either a poor or good experience in school. These feelings of "what school was" influence many parents' attitudes toward schools today. Parents' school experiences extend to impressions of teachers as well. Most parents had wonderful teachers in their lives: individuals who were personable, caring role models for the children in their care. Some may have had negative experiences with teachers that were less than wonderful or, in some cases, just plain poor.

As parents encounter teachers and gauge their personalities, opinions are formed based on their experiences or perhaps rumors heard at the local grocery store or hair salon. Care must be taken not to prematurely judge school employees based on possibly biased comments. While most would agree it is helpful if teachers are "friendly," it is even more important that they are, first and foremost, caring, competent educators. A trustworthy, fair teacher can guide a child in a positive direction. A teacher that lacks a strong academic background, compassion, and a high degree of professionalism is a poor role model, even if he or she is exceedingly friendly.

Most children experience a wide range of teacher personalities during their educational career. Each educator's character and qualities add to the child's makeup and, hopefully, a diverse understanding and appreciation for others.

Questions to Consider

What are the teachers' goals for the year?
Listen/look for: clearly defined goals as presented by the teachers; lists of standards on the classroom walls; articulated plans for students

How does the principal describe his or her staff?
Listen/look for: comments such as excellent teaching staff, wonderful group of educators, a staff that truly cares about children, an experienced and professional staff of caring individuals, the kind of teachers I would like my child to have

Do staff members say "hello" when passing parents in the hallway?
Listen/look for: kind words of welcome: "Hello," "Good morning," "How are you?" "Nice to see you Mrs. _____," "Thank you for coming, Mr. _____."

Do you see teachers and administrators chatting with students?
Listen/look for: educators and support staff taking time to listen to and talk with students; laughing and chatting between students and adults; friendly conversations between adults and children

Do the teachers seem compassionate with the children?
Listen/look for: teachers taking the time to explain things to students; correction being given in a positive manner; good eye contact; treatment of children as individuals with feelings and emotions

Are teachers willing to help the children beyond routine class times?
Listen/look for: teachers staying after class to talk with students; staff members sitting with students working on problems; teachers listening to students that appear to be upset; teachers setting up after-school programs to help students

Are teachers friendly when encountered outside of school?
Listen/look for: recognition of the parents as partners in dealing with children; smiles and acknowledgement of the parent; good eye contact; saying hello to children when encountered at the store, mall, on the street

How Do the School Rules Affect the School Climate?

Rules are a necessary part of school operation. As much as we would like to think that all students come to school ready to learn, anxious to cooperate with teachers, and showing respect for other students, it is an unrealistic expectation. Rules, like laws in the community, maintain order and provide the structure and stability an organization needs.

However, rules should be conscientiously developed, clearly communicated, and fairly administered. Every child should know the rules and the reasons for each rule's existence. Every parent should also be aware of the rules within the school and the consequences for violation. Together with school officials, parents can help teach children proper behavior that will have a direct effect on the school climate.

Schools should develop student handbooks and parent handbooks that outline basic rules students are expected to follow. Questions related to these rules should be openly discussed and clarifications given so that both parents and students are fully conscious of both the rules and the consequences.

Questions to Consider

How are rules formulated and by whom?
Listen/look for: committee of parents and teachers; student input; valid reasons for the rules; legality of rules

What information is covered in the student and parent handbooks?
Listen/look for: student responsibilities, attendance policies, athletics rules, health-related issues, transportation policies, grading policies, student rights, emergency regulations, general information

What do students say about school rules?
Listen/look for: fair, makes me feel safe, reasonable, okay rules, keeps the kids from bothering me, easily understood; posters outlining school rules

Are school rules worded in positive terms?
Listen/look for: "Please Walk" rather than "Don't Run," "Please Remain Quiet" rather than "No Talking," "Please Remain Seated" rather than "No Standing"

Do students appear to talk freely and walk in a relaxed manner in the hallways?
Listen/look for: casual conversations; smiles and laughter; students talking in a manner that demonstrates a spirit of camaraderie

Who assigns school detention and suspension and for what reasons?
Listen/look for: teacher detention as opposed to office detention; suspension numbers (as indicated in state reports); reasons mentioned for suspension of students; why detention is assigned

What does the school's latest state report on violence indicate?
Listen/look for: a listing of violent incidents as indicated on state reports (many states require school districts to submit reports concerning student behavior); reference to reports on the Internet; numbers of suspensions, weapons violations

Are Parents Welcome in the School?

Parents should support the school both financially and emotionally. Parents have a right to expect school personnel to treat them in a manner that reflects a shared concern for children. Respect for parents should be displayed through a caring and polite office staff that meets and deals with parents' concerns in a professional and thoughtful way. Courteous discussion of parental inquiries and timely handling of issues are necessary for a school to be considered parent friendly.

Many schools not only welcome parents but also encourage parent volunteers. Parents can provide the extra pair of helpful hands at lunchtime, offer individual tutoring, or serve as a teacher helper. Along with extending the welcome mat for parents that visit the school, respect must be shown to telephone callers. A friendly welcome, a courteous response, and a willingness to help are signs of a school staff that wants to gain and maintain community support.

Questions to Consider

How are parents welcomed to the school?
Listen/look for: welcome signs for visitors; clear directional signs; recognition as a visitor; a friendly hello and may I help you; asked what they could do for you, politely shown where to sign in, and given a visitor badge; invited to have a seat; helped in a timely manner; thanked for your interest

Are there parent volunteers in the school?
Listen/look for: parent helpers in the library, cafeteria, office, classrooms; signs indicating the welcoming of parent volunteers; indications that volunteers are valued

What kind of reception do parents receive when they call the school?
Listen/look for: courteous phone welcome; informed whom you were speaking with; prompt response to questions or connected to the requested party quickly

Are inquiries and questions responded to in a timely manner?
Listen/look for: reasonable length of time for connection to requested party; knowledgeable response to questions; enough information; willingness to meet to discuss the concern at another time

Is adequate parking provided for visiting parents?
Listen/look for: clear signs indicating visitor parking; adequate parking spaces for visitors; reserved spaces for visitors; parking lots clear of snow; salted parking lots and walkways; clearly identified entry points to the building

Is there an open house or other type of welcoming event for parents?
Listen/look for: open house signs; posters of upcoming evening events (concerts, PTA meetings, school orientations)

Is there an orientation meeting for new parents?
Listen/look for: dates of orientation meetings for new students and their parents; invitation to attend orientation meetings as a new parent in the school

Is there an active PTA or PTO organization in the school?
Listen/look for: posters of upcoming PTA meetings; a listing of PTA officers; reference to the PTA; PTA newsletters for parents

Does the school have Doughnuts for Dad, Muffins for Mom, Grandparents' Day, or similar programs?
Listen/look for: special days and events designed to involve parents in the school; other areas where interested parents, grandparents, or siblings could become a part of the school

SCHOOL SAFETY

In today's world, the safety of children is one of the most important concerns of parents and educators. The school, while attempting to maintain a welcoming climate for students and the public, must institute procedures that enhance the ability to protect the school population.

In order for schools to maintain adequate safety for students and staff members and to enable school personnel to take appropriate action when needed, some security approaches, techniques, and methods must be kept confidential. Sharing details of internal security methods could jeopardize the safety of the school building and could breech the emergency response procedures that exist.

School safety is everyone's responsibility: principal, teacher, support staff, central office administration, school board, student, and parent. Because of recent attacks and intensified attention to potential threats to the school community, many schools have implemented strategies designed to strengthen school security. These security measures have resulted in added expense and increased changes in both the training of staff members and school operating procedures.

Some schools have implemented procedures including visitor sign-ins, visitor badges, employee ID badges, student ID badges, locked doors, security cameras, metal detectors, extended perimeters, emergency drills, evacuation plans, cooperative interaction with police, and panic alarms. But these measures, even when used consistently, do not guarantee a totally safe school. Irate adults or disturbed students remain a threat to any school, regardless of the valiant efforts of school administrators.

Parents should inquire if security methods are in place within the school. Administrators should be willing to discuss the basic operation of their safety procedures and the priority of safety in their school plans. "How will you guard my child's safety?" is a valid question and one that must be answered for a parent to have confidence in the school.

Questions to Consider

Does the school have a "zero tolerance" policy?

Listen/look for: what "zero tolerance" means; how it is applied; if you can have a copy of the policy; does the principal have discretion? If not, why not?

What security programs are operating in the school?

Listen/look for: cameras installed in the lobby, in the parking lot, around the school; a DARE program; presence of a security guard; a sign-in process; a badge for visitors; a buzzer system for access to the building; restricted access to the building without clearance

How many and what types of drills have been conducted?

Listen/look for: regular fire drills; tornado drills; variety of drills; involvement of the fire department in drills; mention of police activity in the school

What security training is provided for teachers?

Listen/look for: in-service training for staff on security measures; type of training provided; last time training took place; response of staff during drills or actual emergencies

What was the latest emergency situation and how was it handled?

Listen/look for: last emergency that took place in the building (parents need to realize that confidentiality issues may preclude specifics); the response time of the emergency personnel; what the school officials learned as a result of the emergency; critiques of past emergencies; steps to improve

Are parents required to sign in and wear a visitor badge?

Listen/look for: requirement to sign in; requirement to wear a visitor badge; need to sign out when leaving; (if not given a badge) did staff in the building notice that you were not wearing a badge?

Is peer mediation offered in the school?

Listen/look for: mention of conflict resolution programs in the school; mention of peer mediation; posting of peer mediation forms and instruction related to steps to take to resolve conflict; mention of peer mediation on the public address system; a listing of peer mediation in the student handbook

Are book bags allowed in the school? Are they searched?
Listen/look for: the presence of book bags when students enter the building; the carrying of book bags between classes; the type of book bags permitted (solid canvas or see-through netting); the use of metal detectors to screen book bags entering the school

Can all classroom doors be locked from the inside?
Listen/look for: the ability of classroom doors to be locked from inside the classroom; the events that might initiate a lockdown and locking of all doors; how library, gym, and other large group instructional areas are locked down

Is there a buzzer at the front entrance?
Listen/look for: a buzzer system at the front door; the locking of all other doors; the use of a camera in addition to the buzzer system; the availability of a staff member to monitor the entrance of visitors; the ability of the school to ascertain the justifiable reason for visitors entering the building

What Procedures Are in Place to Protect the Children?

All schools care about the safety of the children in their care. At the same time, each school has unique characteristics and needs. To be considered secure, the school must have procedures and practices in place that safely transport the children to school, protect them during school hours, and secure their safe return home. Such protection, by necessity, involves the bus drivers and the school staff.

Bus drivers should be trained to deal with safety issues on their buses, just as teachers are trained to handle emergencies within the school. Drivers should be knowledgeable about first aid, be aware of dangers in and around the bus, and be ever alert to potential dangers related to student custody. In-service programs should be provided for bus drivers so they can learn about and rehearse appropriate procedures in the areas of immediate care, contact with police, response to kidnapping attempts, and care of students that are emotionally upset or injured.

All school employees must be trained to deal with a wide range of emergencies and dangerous situations. As adults responsible for hundreds of children, they should be well versed in protocols related to any real or potential danger.

Principals should not only be prepared to respond to emergencies at a moment's notice but should also be continually on the alert to prevent emergencies from occurring in the first place. The planning and development of strategies to be implemented in the event of any type of serious situation is crucial. Firsthand knowledge of police procedures and the need to cooperate with first responders is a key element in maintaining the safety of the school population.

Parents also share in the responsibility for school safety. Following the security rules of the school, entering at the proper entrance, cooperating with office staff in signing in and obtaining a visitor badge, going to and remaining in the appointed area of the building, and supporting teacher directions in the event of an emergency are critical points where parents can be helpful.

Questions to Consider

Are there safety procedures on the school buses?
Listen/look for: training for all bus drivers on dealing with emergencies on buses; police work with bus drivers to provide education relative to procedures during hostage situations

Are there safety patrols to help guide students that walk to school?
Listen/look for: safety patrols assist students that ride buses and walk to and from school; safety patrols are supervised by professional staff; safety patrols are taught how to assist children crossing the street; selection of safety patrol members is based on teacher recommendation

What kind of safety training do bus drivers and school staff members receive?
Listen/look for: how extensive the training is for all support staff; if educational assistants, aides, clerical staff, custodians, janitorial staff, bus drivers, and other nonprofessional school staff are well versed in safety procedures; what agency provides the training to the school staff

Can you describe the type of programs used to train staff members?
Listen/look for: is the staff trained in CPR; is the staff trained in first aid; is the staff trained in the use of a cardiac defibrillator

Does the school have a trained crisis response team?
Listen/look for: does a crisis response team exist in the school; how many staff members serve on the team; do they have regular training sessions; have they developed a crisis response manual; have they participated in emergency drills, tabletop exercises, and simulations

Are psychological services available to children in the event of a crisis?
Listen/look for: when is the school psychologist in the building; what role does she or he play in emergency situations; can the psychologist be available to meet with students experiencing stress or trauma; can additional psychologists be called on for help

What can a parent do to promote safety in the school?
Listen/look for: what role does the parent play in school safety; can parents volunteer to help in an emergency; are parents needed to assist in the event of an evacuation; what can a parent do in a crisis

What clearances do staff members have?
Listen/look for: if staff members have Act 34 clearances (criminal background) or Act 32 clearances (child molestation); if staff members are regularly screened for TB; if staff members receive flu shots

In the event of a terrorist threat, what would the school do?
Listen/look for: an outline of plans that exist in response to a terrorist attack; if the school would be shut down; if the school can be made secure against intruders; if there is water on hand in the event students are sequestered; if students would be sent home in the event of an attack

Is the School Secure during the School Day?

Foremost in the development of a safe school environment is the facility itself. All exterior doors should be locked after the children are inside. If a reliable locking system does not exist on every door, staff members should be continually alert to the unauthorized entry of individuals through unsecured doors (and improvements should be budgeted for). Care must be taken that visitors, when leaving the building, do not exit through secure exits, leaving doors unlocked. This breech in the security of a school building can render all other security measures useless. Periodic monitoring by custodian or administrative staff members should be routine, and door alarms should be installed to signal unauthorized exit.

Teachers in classrooms must be on guard to respond to any emergency that might occur during the day. They should have emergency packets prepared and readily available if needed. All staff members should know the proper procedures to follow depending on the type of emergency. In some cases a lockdown may be required. In others it may be necessary to evacuate the building using established exit routes. Teachers are expected to remain calm in the face of an emergency, making the safety of their children their highest priority.

The administration should continually monitor the school hallways, offices, and classrooms because dangerous situations can erupt anywhere within the school. It is advisable that all administrators carry walkie-talkies and cell phones in order to contact the office or emergency personnel. Knowing what to do, and what not to do, should be an instinctive reaction. Taking time to check a crisis manual during an emergency wastes time, delays decisions, and can result in additional injury or death.

Questions to Consider

Are all exterior doors secured? (Try to open one.)
Listen/look for: all doors are locked after the children enter; even when locked, all doors can be opened from the inside to evacuate the building; no one can enter the building except through the designated entrance door

Are adults picking up children required to show identification?
Listen/look for: proper identification is required for anyone picking up a student from school; in order to pick a child up from school, the adult's name must be listed on the emergency card; the school keeps a complete list of custody issues and abides by the court orders; in the event of a problem, police are called to mitigate the situation

Are fire extinguishers properly charged and ready for emergency use?
Listen/look for: fire extinguishers are regularly checked for proper contents and pressure; fire extinguishers are placed in clearly designated locations; all staff are trained in the operation of fire extinguishers; the fire department is called to the school for any fire, regardless of the size

Are exits clearly marked and well lit?
Listen/look for: exit signs are properly placed and checked for proper operation; all exterior doors have emergency exit lights; all fire exits are clear of debris and obstructions

Is the parking lot monitored during the day and at dismissal?
Listen/look for: cameras monitor the parking lots before, during, and after school hours; video film is kept for review each day; incidents observed as dangerous are immediately investigated by administrative staff; all cameras are routinely monitored

Can unescorted parents walk around inside the building?
Listen/look for: no one is permitted to walk around inside the building without signing in and receiving a visitor badge; any visitor found without a badge is escorted to the office; no exceptions are made to the rule; all staff wear identification badges; any student that sees an individual without a badge is instructed to tell a staff member at once

If given approval ask, "Can anyone just walk around inside the school?"
Listen/look for: there are no exceptions to the sign-in and badge rule

Do teachers move into the hallways between class periods to monitor students?
Listen/look for: staff members are instructed to monitor the hallways outside their classrooms at all times; between classes teachers are requested to step into the hallways to supervise students; all staff members are responsible for the supervision of all children anywhere in the school

Is the office centrally located, making it easily accessible in the event of an emergency?
Listen/look for: the office is easily accessible from all parts of the building; teachers have a method to contact the office in the event of an

emergency; in the event of an emergency office personnel can respond quickly to the scene of the incident

Are hallways clean and clear of obstructions that might interfere with movement?
Listen/look for: custodial staff maintain hallways so that furniture, boxes, and other material do not block movement of students; all doorways are free of items that could jeopardize the safety of children in an evacuation; staff is instructed to inform the office if any item is found to interfere with student movement

Are emergency exits clearly designated and evacuation routes marked?
Listen/look for: every classroom has a fire exit sign in place; all emergency exits are clearly marked; all staff members are aware of the evacuation routes in the event of an emergency

What Do the Children Do in an Emergency?

During an emergency, it is normally sufficient for elementary children to follow the directions of the teacher. Seldom, if ever, are elementary children separated from and devoid of supervision from trained school personnel. Children should be trained to remain quiet, respond to the adult's directions without question, and proceed as instructed in an orderly fashion. The practice of fire drills over the years has helped to instill, within the minds of elementary children, the need to listen to the teacher and move quietly and quickly as directed. Similar procedures need to be followed in other emergencies.

In middle school, junior high, or high school, children may at times be without direct supervision (in the hallways, at lunch, in a locker room). Children at these higher grade levels should be instructed to respond to danger in one of two ways. If an adult is present, the directions of the school staff member are to be followed exactly as given. If the children are not in a position to be directed by an adult, they may have to respond to a situation on their own. Because of this, it is imperative that children of all ages be taught commonsense rules regarding reactions to dangerous activities.

Unusually loud noises, unnaturally fast movement, noise that sounds like gunfire, yelling, and obvious fighting situations should immediately alert the child to take defensive action. This defensive action might include running away, moving behind a secure obstruction (wall, pillar, tree), or dropping to the floor. Such defensive reactions should be part of a child's awareness training to be called on regardless of the location, in or out of school.

I personally observed one serious situation where not only children but also their parents disregarded defensive reaction to potential danger. Recently, while shopping at a local mall, I observed a large man run from a department store only to be tackled by two other individuals. This was followed by the men scuffling and wrestling in the center of the mall concourse. I instinctively stepped behind a nearby pillar, maintained visual contact, and called to a store clerk to notify security. The scuffle continued for approximately four minutes while passersby, hand in hand with their children, formed a circle around the three brawling men. The event, while ending without harm to any onlookers, could have proven deadly before the shoplifter was eventually subdued and escorted away. Had he produced a weapon or been knocked into the crowd, it would most likely have resulted in serious injury to many others. Case in point: Parents need to explain to children and demonstrate commonsense reactions in the face of potential danger.

Questions to Consider

Have students been instructed in escape and evade procedures?
Listen/look for: staff members have instructed students on the proper procedures to follow in the event of an emergency; students are told to follow the instruction of a school staff member at all times

Should a student run from the school when threatened?
Listen/look for: in many cases, when under armed attack, it is best to run away in a zigzag manner, keeping solid objects between you and the assailant; students are to raise their hands when confronted by police to indicate that they are not the attacker

Are there regularly planned practices and drills that include children?
Listen/look for: fire drills, tornado drills, and evacuation drills involve children; some other drills *may* include children, but it is usually recommended that elementary school children not participate in mock emergency drills

Are children instructed to "drop and cover" in the event of weather-related emergencies?
Listen/look for: preplanning for severe weather and other types of natural disasters has helped teach children the proper procedures to follow; students are instructed to drop to the floor and cover their heads to protect themselves from flying glass (tornados and high winds); students are routinely evacuated to areas of the building where glass windows and large expanses are minimized

Do high school students know what to do in an emergency? (Ask one.)
Listen/look for: high school students are normally prepared to seek shelter behind objects in the event of a dangerous situation; they are told to attempt to escape the area whenever possible, keeping large objects (trees, buildings) between themselves and the danger; students are told to run in a zigzag fashion away from the danger

Is there a safe shelter for the children in the school?
Listen/look for: there is a safe area underground for shelter in the event of a tornado; students are evacuated away from classroom windows and into the hallways to avoid flying glass; restrooms provide a more secure shelter than classrooms in weather-related emergencies

What strategies have they been taught?
Listen/look for: drop and cover; evade and run in a zigzag fashion; keep large objects between you and the danger; seek cover behind solid objects; do not wait for a friend; run out of the building to escape danger with your hands in the air

Do teachers speak in normal tones during emergencies or must they raise their voices to be heard?
Listen/look for: through practice, students know to remain quiet in an emergency; staff members know they must maintain a calm and orderly

control during emergencies; normally staff members need only speak in slightly higher volume during a crisis

Are Teachers and Principals Trained to Respond to an Emergency?

Professional educators and other educational staff members should be trained in a wide range of emergency procedures. Teachers must be prepared to react to accidents in the classroom as simple as a student cut by broken glass or as serious as a sniper on a nearby water tower. School districts must train all staff members to react appropriately to the degree of threat and in the correct manner. In-service training by local police departments, emergency response personnel, school psychologists, and other individuals knowledgeable about children and emergency situations is a must. Critical incident practices and drills are important if staff members are to respond without confusion and misunderstanding. The old saying "Practice makes perfect" is applicable here because procedures and protocols not rehearsed and practiced are often confusing or, at the worst, disregarded, resulting in the injury or death of children.

Questions to Consider

How is the staff trained and how often?
Listen/look for: actual drills are conducted that are as realistic as possible; new staff members and substitutes go through an orientation that includes emergency procedures; even the principal is tested in his or her knowledge of protocols; drills are conducted every quarter, and each drill is critiqued and improvements made

Are tabletop exercises, drills, and simulations conducted for all staff?
Listen/look for: all staff members, including clerical, janitorial, and support staff, are trained in emergency procedures; all employees participate in drills, tabletop exercises, and simulations; all staff members have specific responsibilities in the event of an emergency

Do all staff members have copies of the crisis response manual?
Listen/look for: all staff members have copies of the crisis response manual; manuals are to be located in convenient areas for quick

reference; periodic reviews are conducted for all staff on the use of manuals

What is covered in the crisis response manual?
Listen/look for: crisis manuals contain basic information that describes the immediate steps needed to protect the school population; steps to take to evacuate the building, when to lock down, and when to move to another part of the building are all covered

Who provides the training, and is it internally or externally provided?
Listen/look for: resources for training staff in emergency procedures are selected from local police, fire, and emergency management agencies and the local Intermediate Unit (some states); crisis response counselors are available to work with staff during training

Is there a critical incident plan in place within the school?
Listen/look for: critical incident plans are in place in the school; each plan is designed as a quick reference to follow in the event of an emergency; the plan outlines the basic response protocols for staff members to follow

Does the crisis team meet to plan for emergencies?
Listen/look for: the crisis team meets regularly to discuss procedures to follow in the event of an emergency; the crisis team sometimes conducts tabletop exercises to test their readiness to meet any crisis that might occur

Is security a high priority to the principal?
Listen/look for: security is taken very seriously at the school; the increase in reported school emergencies has resulted in more emphasis being placed on safety, security, and protection of the school population in recent years; nothing is more important to principals than a safe environment within the school

Do Police Ever Become Involved in the School?

Police and other emergency personnel are crucial members of the school safety team. Police, by their very nature, need to be relied on to deescalate dangerous situations. On arrival, the police take control and follow agreed upon protocols to deal with the situation (normally through a unified command system). The school administrator, of course, would support their efforts by supplying maps of the school, information relevant to the danger, and guidance related to students and staff members involved (see memorandum of understanding).

Police are placing their lives on the line when responding to emergency situations and need the cooperation and support of school officials. Administrators must assist police by accurately ascertaining if the school facility has been cleared through a well-developed accounting system for all students and staff members. This reduces the need for first responders to unnecessarily search the facility.

Questions to Consider

Under what circumstances would the police be called to the school?
Listen/look for: the agreement between the police and school district outlines the reasons police might be called to the school; anytime 911 is called, police and fire rescue respond to the school; cases that involve a criminal act mandate the involvement of police

When was the last time police were called to the school and why?
Listen/look for: valid reasons for police to have been called (no names should be divulged)

What role do police play in school emergencies?
Listen/look for: once police are summoned to the school they are in charge of the situation; school staff support and assist police once they are on the scene; police may arrest, search, or sequester students as part of an ongoing investigation; the school officials assist in maintaining any crime scene that might exist

What is the average response time of emergency agencies during a crisis?
Listen/look for: response time to school emergencies depends on a number of variables: distance the police are from the building, the time of day and amount of traffic, the number of patrol cars on the highway, and the level of danger

Do police have maps and floor plans of the school building?

Listen/look for: a "to go" box (taken in the event of an evacuation) contains maps, floor plans, and utility shutoffs for each building; often schools submit maps and floor plans to local police for their quick reference; maps and floor plans are kept in the office for reference when needed

Are police familiar with the layout of the building?

Listen/look for: local police sometimes use the school facility for practices during the weekends; police review building layout with school administrators; while police like to know the various sections of a building before entering, they are trained to enter, gain control, and mitigate dangerous situations

Do the school and police have a memorandum of understanding agreement?

Listen/look for: there is an understanding between the school and police on protocols required in emergencies; agreements with police and fire agencies are reviewed and updated regularly

Are Emergency Drills Conducted Regularly?

As stated earlier, to be effective and to reduce confusion, emergency drills should be conducted on a regular basis in all schools. Most parents remember fire drills when they were in school. Today, more is needed. Drills related to all sorts of unexpected emergencies should be conducted. Staff must be ready to respond to such drills at any time, treating each practice as the real thing. Only through rehearsals can areas needing improvement be discovered and corrective measures taken. Mistakes discovered during a drill can easily be improved upon; mistakes during an actual emergency could have devastating results.

Questions to Consider

How many emergency drills are conducted yearly?

Listen/look for: monthly fire drills (even in the summer when students are in the building); tornado drills biannually; crisis drills quarterly or at least two times per year

How are students accounted for during an emergency?

Listen/look for: teachers are responsible for accounting for all students during emergencies; all teachers are to take roll books with them if they evacuate the building; the names of unaccounted-for students are reported to the administrator at once; all restrooms, classrooms, and other areas are searched in the event of an emergency

Are staff members provided with updates on current emergency procedures?

Listen/look for: any suggested changes or improvements in existing emergency procedures are conveyed to all staff; principals are responsible for maintaining the most current protocols for emergencies

What types of drills are conducted?

Listen/look for: fire, tornado, sniper, armed intruder, hostage, shots fired, structural collapse, severe weather, earthquake, high water, flooding, hurricane, being sequestered, child abduction, missing child, bus accident, death of a teacher, death of a student, and so on

How are students and staff notified of a drill?

Listen/look for: normally a public address announcement is made to initiate a drill; sometimes code words are used to alert staff members to the beginning of a drill; sometimes drills are announced, but at other times they may be unannounced

Do fire officials monitor and occasionally conduct emergency drills?

Listen/look for: fire officials routinely initiate and monitor at least one fire drill per year; when invited, fire and police officials will try to attend drills and offer suggestions for improvement

How are disabled students transported during an emergency drill?

Listen/look for: disabled individuals are cared for during a drill or actual emergency; individual staff members are assigned to assist disabled individuals to safe areas; in the event that wheelchairs are not operational, a two-man carry is used to transport disabled individuals; in all cases disabled individuals are transported out of harm's way

Do students and staff members take drill procedures seriously?

Listen/look for: all staff members know the seriousness of emergency drills; students are continually reminded that drills are conducted for their protection and safety; teachers require students to remain quiet and to follow directions during drills; students found to be uncooperative during drills are referred to the office for discipline

Can a parent observe the next emergency drill?
Listen/look for: we do not announce our drills to the general public; individual parents with a special interest in observing a drill can arrange to be present at a regularly scheduled drill

When was the last time a drill was conducted?
Listen/look for: fire drill within the last month; tornado drill usually in the fall and spring; other drills as scheduled

What would you do differently to improve the next drill?
Listen/look for: always room for improvement; perhaps improved response time; better communication with staff; better behavior of some students; better cooperation of visitors in the building

SEVERE WEATHER CONDITIONS

Every school, in every state, experiences weather-related situations. Hurricanes occur in the south, tornados in the Midwest, snowstorms in the east, and earthquakes in the west. Floods, severe weather, and high winds confront schools everywhere. The procedures in place to meet such weather-related situations could be a great help in calming parents' concerns and maintaining the school's mission of educating children.

Many schools have delayed starts if weather forecasts or current conditions warrant postponing normal starting times. Early dismissals can be implemented if forecasts of changes in the weather would hamper regular dismissal times. Cancellation of school for the entire day is a possibility if weather predictions or current conditions would jeopardize the safety of students or staff members.

While such changes in the school's normal operating times can cause disruptions in parents' schedules, the need to protect children is paramount. Once again, parent convenience is not a substitute for the safety of children.

Questions to Consider

Do all schools have operating weather alert radios?

Listen/look for: weather radios are located in every school office in the district; backup batteries are in place in the event of an electrical outage; weekly alerts are monitored; a staff member is assigned to listen to and report any weather alerts

Is there a secure area for protection from tornados and severe weather?

Listen/look for: there is an underground shelter for staff and students (limited number of schools); students are to go to the hallway and cover their heads; students are moved away from windows and out of areas with expansive roofs (gym, auditorium); children can be evacuated to a building next door (limited number of buildings)

Is there an emergency supply of water in the school?

Listen/look for: a limited water supply is on hand; water is on hand for drinking purposes if school is extended a few hours; water supplies must be replaced monthly; normally school children are not held at school for any great length of time

What happens if a school bus encounters severe weather on the way home?

Listen/look for: drivers are instructed to take the children to the nearest secure site; all buses have radios to summon help; drivers are trained to respond to changes in the weather and driving conditions (snow, ice, strong winds, high water)

How do parents receive word of an emergency?

Listen/look for: normally parents hear of emergencies via the radio or television; it is impossible for the school to contact every parent in the event of a schoolwide emergency; parents should not go to the school unless school and police officials have authorized it; parents should not call the school regarding emergency situations

Who makes weather-related decisions that alter school times?

Listen/look for: often the maintenance department, superintendent, and police confer and decide if school should be held or dismissed early; cancellation decisions must be made early before school to avoid some children being transported

What provisions are made for working parents in case of early dismissal?
Listen/look for: schools are first and foremost concerned about the safety of children; parents are notified as early as possible regarding school delays or cancellations; parents should have a backup plan for days when the school is closed or there is an early dismissal and they must be at work

Is the windchill factor considered in adjusting school times?
Listen/look for: windchill factors influence the decision to close school; when large numbers of students walk to school or must wait outside for school buses the windchill is a major factor

Does the school have emergency backup generators in the event of a power blackout?
Listen/look for: the school has backup generators for limited lighting during power outages; generators are regularly serviced and maintained for emergency use

Why Is School Sometimes Delayed, Dismissed, or Canceled?

School may be canceled for a variety of valid reasons. The loss of electricity, inadequate water supply, excessive snowfall, ice storms, police orders, or health-related reasons might result in cancellation of school. Most states require a specific number of school days (or a certain number of school hours) per year. When school is canceled, in many cases, these days must be made up at a later time. Because of this, district officials are reluctant to unnecessarily cancel school unless conditions warrant such action. The use of delayed starts has provided an alternative to outright cancellation of school by permitting a few extra hours in the morning to decide if schools can be open.

When weather conditions warrant it or some other type of emergency arises, the school superintendent may decide, in the interest of safety, to delay, dismiss, or cancel school. Most districts fully realize that early dismissal can cause confusion and disrupt parents' work schedules. But the safety of the students is the foremost consideration. Schools may initiate a delayed start or early dismissal for such events as forecasted ice storms, predicted severe weather, community or national emergencies, or other out-of-the ordinary circumstances.

Questions to Consider

What is a delayed start?

Listen/look for: a delayed start of school is a method whereby the beginning of the school day is postponed for a certain period of time, often two hours; it allows school officials, police, and other officials time to decide if it is safe to conduct school that day; when a two-hour delayed start is announced, it means that classes are either delayed two hours or may possibly be canceled for the day; in a delayed start the normal dismissal time is maintained

How are parents notified of a delayed start?

Listen/look for: when weather is threatening, parents are to tune into their local radio or television stations for news related to the possibility of a delayed start or cancellation of school for the day

What is early dismissal?

Listen/look for: early dismissal is a process whereby students are released from school earlier than the normal dismissal time

Why is an early dismissal authorized?

Listen/look for: early dismissal may be authorized for a variety of reasons: predicted ice storms, impending snow storms, possible dangerous situations that early dismissals would avoid; most school administrators realize that early dismissals can be upsetting to parents but the children's safety is foremost in their thinking

Who can tell the schools to dismiss early?

Listen/look for: normally the school superintendent makes the final decision as to the need for an early dismissal; decisions are often based on recommendations from local police, emergency agencies, the department of highways, and other public agencies

When is the decision made to dismiss early?

Listen/look for: depending on the organization of the district, early dismissal is usually decided late in the morning or in early afternoon; if a district uses buses for several runs (high school then middle school and finally elementary) decisions must be made to coincide with the availability of buses

Do students have to make up the time when they have an early dismissal?

Listen/look for: normally students do not have to make up time because of an early dismissal

Will there ever be an early dismissal?

Listen/look for: early dismissals are sometimes required; often early dismissals are implemented because of an impending change in the weather such as a predicted ice storm or other severe weather conditions; sometimes it is necessary to dismiss early because of an internal problem at the school such as a loss of heat, water, or electricity

How early will parents be contacted about school cancellation?

Listen/look for: in some cases predicted severe weather will result in school being canceled the evening before; in most cases the determination of a school cancellation is not made until early in the morning; once again, parents should listen to local media when conditions make school delay or cancellation a possibility

What happens if the weather is too bad for the children to walk home?

Listen/look for: children will not be forced to walk home from school in severe weather; often children are sequestered at school until weather conditions lessen or parents come to school to pick them up; children at school will be safely supervised

STUDENT ILLNESS

Most schools keep emergency cards that list parents' home and work phone numbers as well as alternative contact persons. Individual children's emergencies including personal injury, serious illness, or other common concerns are most likely communicated to parents by telephone. Schools are reluctant to make decisions regarding a child's health without parent permission and acknowledgement. Because of this, it is imperative that parents keep both their home and work phone numbers and authorized backup phone numbers current.

In the event of a schoolwide emergency, the news media are usually the most rapid means used to notify parents. Parents cannot be called individually because of the sheer number involved. Additionally, parents are requested not to call the school because incoming calls tie up phone lines that may be needed. Coming to the school in response to police scanners can create situations that not only interfere with emergency personnel's ability to assist at the scene but also may endanger lives. The best advice in the event of a schoolwide emergency is to listen to the media, go to the location designated by the school authorities, and await information from the police. As difficult as it may be for parents, it is usually best to allow the professionals to do their jobs without interference.

Questions to Consider

How do teachers handle a sick child?
Listen/look for: normally when a child becomes ill, the child is taken to the health room, administrators are notified, and the parent is contacted; in severe cases the parent is requested to come and get the child, or 911 is called; the school is not a hospital and can only administer first aid until help arrives

How is a parent contacted if a child becomes ill at school?
Listen/look for: emergency cards kept on file are used to contact parents in the event of a child's illness; it is important for parents to keep emergency cards current with present phone numbers and the names of individuals authorized to pick up their children

Will the school staff provide first aid?
Listen/look for: many school staff members are trained in first aid; the nurse is authorized to administer first aid; normally, depending on the emergency, 911 is called and then the parent

How long would it take for the ambulance to reach the school?
Listen/look for: response time of an ambulance to a school emergency depends on a number of factors: weather, road conditions, flow of traffic, distance from the school

What if a parent is unavailable to come to the school?
Listen/look for: parents are requested to fill out emergency cards to be used in the event they cannot be contacted or cannot come to the school; parents should arrange for a friend or relative to serve as a backup when they are unable to come to the school; students will be released only to individuals with authorization from parents

Can a parent call the school and have another adult pick his child up?
Listen/look for: in most schools parents must name, in writing, the individual(s) authorized to pick their child up at school; individuals coming to school to pick up a student must show proper identification and be listed on the child's emergency card; *schools will not release students to unauthorized individuals*

If so, how does the school know it was the parent that called?
Listen/look for: schools will not release students to unauthorized individuals

Will the school call a second number if the parent cannot be reached?
Listen/look for: the school is usually willing to attempt to contact anyone listed on the emergency card when a child is injured or ill; all phone numbers and authorized individuals must be kept current

Can the school nurse keep and administer medication for bee stings, allergic reactions, and other health-related dangers?
Listen/look for: most schools will permit parents to leave emergency medications for authorized use; a doctor's prescription is required for the dispensing of any medication at school

Who accompanies a child if transportation to the hospital is necessary?
Listen/look for: normally the nurse will accompany an injured child to the hospital; the principal may accompany or follow the ambulance to the hospital

Where do parents go to seek information during an emergency?
Listen/look for: listening to the radio or watching television can provide parents with current information about school emergencies; often school district officials will meet with and respond to parents concerning individual school emergencies; parents should not come to the school as it may create additional danger or interfere with emergency procedures in place

SCHOOL EMERGENCIES

Emergencies have always occurred in schools. Today, if the media are to be believed, there are more reported incidents of shootings, bullying, intimidation, and sexual abuse than in the past. Many feel the influence of television, movies, and music has been instrumental in increasing the degree of student unrest and violence. But regardless of the instigating reasons, there is undoubtedly more attention being focused on potential emergencies in the schools and strategies to mitigate the dangers to children.

Does the School Have an Evacuation Plan?

Many schools today do have evacuation plans. The recent attention to schoolwide events such as Columbine High School and others have encouraged schools to look for host sites to house children until the danger has been mitigated. This is no easy task. Many schools are located a substantial distance from large buildings that might serve as temporary housing for hundreds of children. Individuals living near the school may not welcome or permit the invasion of children into their homes from the school across the street, and buses may take an extended period of time to reach the school. To make matters worse, immediate evacuation may force young children to remain outside without coats in inclement weather. As I said, it is no easy task!

If a school does have an evacuation plan, experts normally think it best if the route is unknown to those outside the school. Individuals intent on doing potential harm to children might use such information. Many schools, however, will advertise the location of host sites so that parents, with proper identification, can pick up children in an orderly manner.

Questions to Consider

Under what circumstances would the school be evacuated?

Listen/look for: the school is evacuated anytime it is safer to be outside the facility rather than inside; many factors influence the decision to evacuate a school: current weather, type of internal danger, distance to the host site; the school is evacuated when it will increase the safety of children and staff members

What happens during inclement weather?

Listen/look for: some schools have adequate host structures nearby; some may call buses to evacuate the building; others may move children to a secure part of the building until buses arrive; some will move children a safe distance from the building (if weather permits)

Who makes the decision to evacuate the school?

Listen/look for: many school principals have the authority to evacuate their school buildings because of the need to vacate without delay; some districts request that principals contact central office personnel before evacuation is initiated; when police or fire officials arrive it is their decision whether to evacuate or remain in the building

How long does it take to evacuate the building?

Listen/look for: for security reasons, times required for evacuations are normally held in confidence by staff administrations

What is the location of the host site in the event of an evacuation?

Listen/look for: many schools do not advertise the location of the host site to avoid possible danger to the students; in some cases the principal may divulge the location but not the route followed to reach the site; listen to the radio and television for the location of the host site in the event of an evacuation

Do students and staff practice evacuation drills?

Listen/look for: all staff members participate in evacuation drills; students are instructed in the proper procedure to follow in an evacuation; students and staff members actually practice going to the host site

How far from the school is the evacuation site?
Listen/look for: normally the evacuation site is near enough to the school to permit easy walking; if the host site is some distance away, buses will transport students

How long does it take for the students to reach the host site?
Listen/look for: the time necessary to reach the host site depends on the weather and the route taken; if buses are used the time will be influenced by the traffic flow, the weather, and the time initially required for buses to arrive at the school

How can a parent pick up her child?
Listen/look for: listen to the local radio and television stations for information relative to picking up your child; police and emergency personnel will know the relocation of children; it is necessary that proper identification be displayed before any child can be picked up at the host site

In a countywide emergency, where would the children be taken?
Listen/look for: schools have backup plans in the event that a disaster takes place over a large area; buses may take children to another school, or the children may be safer remaining at their home school until emergency agencies signal the all clear

Who Monitors the Safety of Students?

The entire school staff is responsible for monitoring the safety of school children. It takes a united team effort to guard the school community against the numerous potential dangers that exist; an alert and watchful professional staff is imperative for a safe school. At the same time, parents must take the responsibility of notifying the school principal if they are aware of any potential danger. The administrator will follow up on such "tips" to determine if the danger is real.

Questions to Consider

Is there a security officer in the school on a regular basis?
Listen/look for: many schools have security officers on site during school hours; some schools depend on the local police for protection;

in many cases security personnel are hired only for general patrols and to notify police of emergency situations

Who checks the condition of the playground equipment? How often?
Listen/look for: playground equipment is checked on a regular basis; normally weekly inspections are completed; dangerous equipment is reported and repaired before the playground is opened for children to use

How often is the nurse in the building?
Listen/look for: most states have a set minimum student–nurse ratio; in some states it is as much as 1,500 students per nurse (PA); often school districts will provide additional health coverage through the use of LPNs (medication administration)

Who administers a child's medication if the nurse is absent?
Listen/look for: in most schools a principal or other responsible staff member will administer prescribed medication to students; often other schools will send a nurse to cover for an absent nurse

Is there a "tip line" for reporting rumors and potential dangers to the principal?
Listen/look for: many schools now have a "tip line" or "hot line" for use in reporting rumors, warning of potential danger, or reporting upcoming events of interest to school officials; care must be taken in following up on all "tips," but school officials usually find such aids useful; the involvement of parents as aware, watchful adults is a great asset to schools

Do administrators and staff members take all threats seriously?
Listen/look for: safety is taken very seriously in schools; principals and teachers normally consider children's safety one of their major responsibilities

What happens if the principal is not in the building when an emergency occurs?
Listen/look for: schools have backup plans and protocols to follow if the principal is out of the building; critical incident teams or lead teachers may be responsible for covering for the principal; in most cases either the principal can return to the building quickly or a principal from a nearby building can come to the school; in all cases schools are never without someone to take charge in the event of an emergency

What about Bomb Threats?

Over the years, bomb threats have disrupted schools from coast to coast. While the actual danger of a bomb being constructed and placed in a school may be considered remote, between 1998 and 2001, sixty-five explosive devices were found in schools. Administrators cannot take chances. The lives of hundreds of children and staff depend on their wise decisions. In many schools, various techniques are employed to intercept bomb threats, and staff members are trained in procedures to follow when receiving such threats. Police are diligent in the pursuit of bomb threats, and schools nationwide prosecute perpetrators to the fullest extent of the law.

Questions to Consider

What procedures are in place in the event there is a telephoned bomb threat?

Listen/look for: all bomb threats are taken seriously; every bomb threat is treated as a real bomb; every person answering an outside phone line is trained in the procedures to follow if a threat is phoned to the school; teachers visually check their rooms; in all cases police are called and the emergency protocol is followed

Are children always evacuated after a bomb threat?

Listen/look for: evacuation of the school building is the decision of the administrator in charge or outlined in the protocols for bomb threats; weather, time of day, and details of the bomb threat may influence the decision to evacuation the building

How far away from the building are students moved?

Listen/look for: children are moved a safe distance from the school building; the exact distance children are moved is normally kept confidential for security reasons

Are teachers trained in bomb threat techniques?

Listen/look for: all staff members are trained in procedures to follow during a bomb threat; in some schools drills are conducted to test staff members' responses to potential bomb threat situations

Are all classroom doors locked at night to deter bomb placement?
Listen/look for: in most schools all classroom doors are locked after school except while being cleaned; only areas open for evening activities are unlocked; either teachers have keys to their rooms or custodians lock and unlock classroom doors daily

What if a bomb is found?
Listen/look for: in the event a bomb is found, police normally withdraw, cordon off the area, and wait until the bomb squad arrives

What if a bomb detonates?
Listen/look for: in the event a bomb detonates, the site becomes a crime scene and police have complete jurisdiction; normally other agencies (fire department, AFT, FBI) become involved

Could a Columbine-Type Incident Happen in the School?

Despite the desire to say, "No, it could never happen at your school," the fact is "Yes, it could!" The one common denominator found in every school shooting from Columbine to Edinboro is the statement from parents and teachers that "I never thought it could happen here!" Regardless of the tireless efforts of well-trained teachers, principals, and support staffs and the support of central office administrators and school boards, no group of individuals and no procedures can ensure the unconditional safety of any school. The most that anyone can do is their best to safeguard the school and its population from harm.

Parents should inquire if the school is taking safety and security seriously and if procedures are in place to make every effort to keep their children out of harm's way.

Questions to Consider

Could a Columbine-type incident happen in the school?
Listen/look for: principals cannot say a criminal act will never take place in their schools; there are measures in place designed to reduce the chances of such an event; staff members are alert to possible dangers and aware of procedures to follow to help prevent such situations

If the answer is yes, what is needed to increase security?
Listen/look for: alert and aware parents are always a great help in preventing school violence; reinforcement of school rules and children reporting potentially dangerous situations, rumors, and gang activity all help reduce school violence

If the answer is no, why not?
Listen/look for: peer mediation, tip lines, conflict resolution programs, clear rules against harassment, DARE programs, guidance programs on peer pressure, and open communication between adults and children help mitigate potentially serous situations

Continue: Are you certain such an event could never happen here?
Listen/look for: all the school district can do is attempt to create a climate where students are listened to, fair rules are consistently administered, and well-developed policies with rational consequences are in place

Are students monitored and counseled about threats and bullying?
Listen/look for: guidance personnel present lessons on conflict resolution; teachers supervise and report any incidents of bullying or threats; peer mediation programs provide an avenue for conflict resolution

Are metal detectors and armed security personnel used to screen students as they enter?
Listen/look for: in some schools armed security guards are posted at the entrance to the building; in some schools the use of metal detectors is not currently considered a necessity

How would the school react if a rumor was circulating that a student had a gun in school?
Listen/look for: every school has a protocol addressing a weapon in school; teachers are required to report the possible existence of a weapon to the principal; the principal normally would notify police; in many cases the student is brought to the office to await the arrival of the police

Are there programs in place to help avoid tension between students?
Listen/look for: peer mediation programs, conflict resolution, anti-bullying, DARE, student assistance programs, and so on

Are harassment cases investigated thoroughly?
Listen/look for: all cases of harassment are considered serious; both parties are interviewed, witnesses are called if necessary, and parents are called; in cases where harassment is verified consequences are administrated

What about Evening Activities and School Safety?

After school hours, the school building takes on a less dynamic stance. Once teachers, the principal, and support staff leave the facility for the day, the primary school employees remaining are normally the custodial staff. Their major responsibility is cleaning the classrooms and preparing the building for the next day of classes. It is usually very difficult for this evening staff to monitor those that enter the building for evening activities. Because of this, schools typically require that specific individuals be responsible for the behavior and actions of their participants during all evening activities.

The resulting problem in some schools is the potential risk of unsupervised, unauthorized persons entering the building for potentially unlawful and criminal reasons. Evening activities have many principals concerned because of the inability to guard the school facility from potential risk. Some efforts that have been taken in some schools include cordoning off hallways with metal screens, employing security guards, and installing security cameras. But many schools often have difficulty justifying the costs involved in the use of technology or additional security staff.

Unguarded schools are more likely to be placed in jeopardy, and the permission given for external groups to use school facilities is worrisome.

Questions to Consider

What safeguards are in place to protect the school after hours?
Listen/look for: normally all interior classroom doors are locked except for when classrooms are being cleaned; in many schools locked steel gates are positioned to cordon off the areas not being used for evening activities; supervisors of evening events are responsible for patrolling

their areas and guarding against individuals intent on doing damage or posing a danger to the school or its population

Could an individual hide a weapon in the school during an after-school event?

Listen/look for: it is always possible for someone to hide a small object in a school; the accessibility of the school building after hours is a concern for all principals; often evening activities are located away from student lockers, restrooms, and classrooms; custodian staff are alert to movement within their building and watch for unauthorized persons within secured areas; supervisors of activities are usually responsible for guarding against weapons and other illegal items entering the building; custodians check the areas before locking the building each night

How do I know the school is safe during an evening event?

Listen/look for: every precaution is taken to protect spectators at evening events; often extra personnel are on duty; police are sometimes stationed at doors and areas of possible danger; metal detectors are sometimes used; emergency generators are operational; cell phones and other emergency equipment is available

Are all exterior doors unlocked during evening events?

Listen/look for: fire code regulations require that doors in the building areas being used for evening activities be unlocked and available for exit in the event of a fire; normally exterior doors are locked from the outside and can be opened through the use of a crash bar from the inside

Are custodians on duty during the weekend?

Listen/look for: in many schools custodial staff is on duty during the weekends for maintenance and cleaning responsibilities; in many schools security systems are installed to protect the facility from intrusion and vandalism; police normally patrol areas around the schools on weekends and in the evening hours

What about Sporting Events and Safety?

Sporting events incur special issues related to school safety. In response, many schools employ extra security personnel and ask staff members to assist in supervision of students and help with crowd control.

Once again, sections of the facility not in use may be screened off as long as emergency exits are not blocked. All classroom doors should be locked to prevent entry. Lights should be on in the building to hamper intruders moving into unauthorized areas, and personnel should be posted in locations where they command a clear view of sensitive areas. Additionally, all exterior lights should be on to disrupt illegal activity.

Questions to Consider

Are police alerted that the event is being held and prepared to respond if needed?

Listen/look for: it is common practice to notify local police when large group meetings or events are planned at schools; increased traffic and the possibility of emergency situations are communicated to police

Are medical staff members on duty during sporting events?

Listen/look for: usually doctors do not attend all sporting events, but coaches and other staff members are specially trained to deal with sports-related injuries and blood spills; cell phones are on hand; emergency resources normally respond rapidly

Are all coaches trained to deal with bloodborne pathogens?

Listen/look for: all school staff members are trained in proper handling of blood-related issues; gloves and other appropriate supplies are stored near every event where there might be a blood spill

What about traffic control at sporting events?

Listen/look for: police or hired security guards often deal with increased traffic flow at sporting events; in some cases spectators are bussed in from other larger parking lots if the school facility cannot accommodate the large number of automobiles

Who monitors the parking lot?

Listen/look for: security guards, teaching staff, police, and representatives of the event being held sometimes monitor parking lots

Who is in charge of crowd control?

Listen/look for: generally the building principal is the coordinator of crowd control; in some cases coaches, supervisors, security personnel, and teachers assist the principal; in the event of a serious crowd control problem police may intervene

Are locker rooms locked before and during games?
Listen/look for: locker rooms are normally locked until they are needed; after games the locker rooms are locked immediately after the teams are finished and then reopened for cleaning; during the games coaches and other school staff members monitor access to the locker rooms

Can disruptive students be kept out of the games?
Listen/look for: students found to be disruptive and in danger of causing harm can be removed from the building; school rules are in effect at all school activities, and thus an enrolled student that misbehaves can be disciplined in accordance with school policy; students on suspension or expelled typically cannot attend school-sponsored activities during the period of punishment

How do you control the behavior of visiting teams and spectators?
Listen/look for: the responsibility of controlling the visiting team is that of the coaches and school authorities of that school; in the event of a disturbance that interferes with the game, the referees may have spectators removed or forfeit the game; police on duty can exercise their police powers and arrest anyone violating the law (trespassing, intoxication, harassment, fighting, violence, vandalism, and so on)

Is Technology Used in the Area of Safety?

The increased use of technology in school security is evident in many schools. Externally, security cameras scan parking lots, exteriors of the building, and outlying buildings. Internally, hallway cameras, electronic scanning of staff badges, and automatic locking devices on doors help protect the school.

In light of this recent increase in technology, school boards have looked at the costs involved in the installation of protective devices. The cost can be very high. In addition, the installation of some security methods necessitates additional staff. Metal detectors without armed security protection are questionable. The use of cameras without assigned individuals to monitor them may lack validity.

Questions to Consider

How does the school protect the exterior of the building during the evenings?

Listen/look for: most schools have extensive lighting to help disrupt vandalism after school hours; community members and parents living near the school can be a great help in reporting unusual activity around the school; police often patrol areas around schools during the evening hours

Are the exterior doors equipped with buzzers to protect against unlawful entry?

Listen/look for: some schools have buzzers connected to exterior doors; some schools have entry lights that signal when the door is ajar; it should be noted that all doors must be unlocked from the inside to meet fire code regulations

Does the school have panic buttons in place to summon police?

Listen/look for: schools have many security devices in place that should not and can not be shared with the community; some schools do have panic buttons to be used to alert police when the school is in danger and phone calls cannot be made

Are security cameras effective?

Listen/look for: security cameras are often very useful in the conviction of criminals that enter the school illegally; with proper monitoring, security cameras are a useful tool in reducing school vandalism; cameras positioned to view the parking lot area have helped reduce student smoking and some gang activity

Are all students required to walk through metal detectors?

Listen/look for: some schools require all students to enter the school through metal detectors; often schools use handheld wands to check for illegal items; particularly at school dances and special events, care must be taken that students are not singled out to be searched, as some state laws forbid profiling students for searches

What happens if a student is caught with a knife or weapon at a metal detector?

Listen/look for: as stated earlier, it is important that every metal detector be manned by an armed security guard; students found to be in possession of a weapon are taken into custody by school officials until police arrive; normally the school will prosecute students and proceed with suspension or, in many cases, expulsion

Are cameras used during the school day?
Listen/look for: some schools monitor areas of the school where possible violent acts might occur; hallways, cafeterias, study halls, lobbies, and parking lots are often under camera surveillance

Are cameras placed on school buses?
Listen/look for: more and more school districts are mounting video cameras on school buses; cameras on buses are useful as a deterrent to violent behavior and can be used as visual proof when there is a denial of misbehavior

How Is the School Protected against Intruders?

Individuals coming to the school with the purpose of doing harm have increased the need for sign-in procedures and screening by office personnel. While it may be difficult to detect adults carrying a weapon (without the use of metal detectors), office staff sensitive to the emotional state of visitors can serve as a screening mechanism. Initiating conversations with visitors and inquiring as to the purpose of the visit can often alert school personnel to potential threats. When concerns exist regarding specific individuals the principal can be called, security personnel alerted, or in the worse case scenario, police contacted. But, to be honest, any individual intent on causing harm to a school population can be difficult to stop without police armed intervention.

The best defense against intruders that are planning disruption or harm to the school is an alert staff, the development of good rapport between parents and school staff, and a principal that seeks to prevent potential problems rather than sit back and wait for them to happen.

Questions to Consider

What steps would you take to stop an adult intent on injuring students?
Listen/look for: in many schools visitors are asked their business before being permitted into the building; once directed to the office to sign in, visitors are screened by office staff so that their emotional status can be

ascertained; if a problem arises or there is reason to believe that an individual is harmful in any way, the principal is called or police are called; in some schools the classroom area is inaccessible without going through the office area

What is a lockdown?
Listen/look for: a lockdown is a method utilized to secure an area to prevent a threatening situation from endangering students and staff members

When is a lockdown used?
Listen/look for: the use of a lockdown depends on the type of danger that exists; one type of lockdown is to lock all exterior doors while classes continue their normal routine (in the case of a bank robbery a few blocks from the school); a second type of lockdown would result in all exterior doors and all classroom doors being locked while classes continue within the rooms (an accident on the playground with ambulances arriving); a third type of lockdown would trigger the immediate locking of all classroom doors and students taking shelter on the floor away from all doors and windows (an intruder in the building)

Can the teachers keep an intruder out of the classrooms?
Listen/look for: most classrooms have locks on the doors that allow teachers to secure them, but it should be noted that classroom doors are normally not metal and keeping out an intruder intent on gaining entry may be impossible; the best approach is to deny an intruder access to the classroom area

Do you have methods to alert police to serious problems in the school?
Listen/look for: local police normally respond very rapidly to school incidents; many schools have panic buttons to summon police (similar to those in banks); school staffs are trained to phone police when any situation appears to be potentially dangerous

Are office staff members trained on what to do in confrontational situations?
Listen/look for: many school staff members are trained in confrontational deescalation and conflict resolution; normally personnel located in the school office can reduce an irate parent's stress level

Is there any way to alert teachers of the necessity to lock their classroom doors?

Listen/look for: most experts recommend that alerts to school personnel be simple and direct; while some schools use codes (code blue, code red), many schools merely make an announcement ("This is a lockdown. All teachers lock all classroom doors."); additionally it is recommended that teachers learn to act on their own when they sense danger or hear activity of a potentially harmful nature

Why can't visitors be "buzzed" into the school?

Listen/look for: in some schools visitors are buzzed into the building, but being buzzed into the building does not guarantee that a visitor is harmless

Why don't you have armed security guards in the building?

Listen/look for: many schools have security guards (armed and unarmed) in the school buildings; security needs such as using metal detectors and patrolling the hallways and parking lots are sometimes best met by trained security personnel

DRUGS IN THE SCHOOL

In today's schools, the possession and use of illegal drugs is an ongoing concern. Parents need to know that the school often reflects the community around it. Thus, if drugs are present in the neighborhood near the school site, it is likely that they are in the school as well. Parents need to work with schools to implement programs and courses that address drug use and then monitor the environment in which children exist. Stiff, fair, and consistently administered rules are a great help. Making certain that students know the consequences of drug use and close, parental monitoring of student activities are vital. Cooperation between parents and the school officials is critical for effective illegal drug prevention. In the final analysis, it is the relationship between parent and child that makes the greatest impact on the behavior of children. Open communication, freedom to express ideas, and the setting of standards are great assets in the building of a healthy foundation necessary to say no to offers of drugs in the community and in the schools.

Questions to Consider

Why can't the principal stop student drug use in the school?

Listen/look for: often drug use in a school reflects the drug use in the community around the school, and as such, the problem goes far beyond the school's ability to control; principals attempt to stem the flow of drugs into the school environment through the use of many programs, techniques, and resources; the best way to stop the spread of drugs in the school is to work as a partner with police and the community to stop drug use

Are there programs in place to reduce drug use?

Listen/look for: most schools have instituted drug awareness programs (DARE) and informative programs for parents and their children, involved police and community resources, and enacted strong consequences for drugs or drug paraphernalia in school

Do you use ex–drug addicts to scare the kids?

Listen/look for: many schools have found the use of ex–drug users as a scare tactic to be unsuccessful; students often look at the ex-users and rationalize that they too can take drugs and go on to successful lives; as a result, many feel that such programs are counterproductive; normally trained teachers conduct the lessons

Have you ever had drug dogs in the school?

Listen/look for: many secondary schools routinely use drug dogs; drug dogs are one tool that has been found helpful in discovering drugs on the person of students or in student lockers and automobiles

Are there drugs in the neighborhood?

Listen/look for: unfortunately, there are some aspects of illegal drug use in most communities; discussions with local police will reveal if a drug culture exists near the school

Is the school a drug area on weekends?

Listen/look for: the monitoring of large school buildings over the weekends can be a difficult task; many school buildings have nooks and crannies that conceal various kinds of inappropriate behavior; many schools hire security personnel to patrol school grounds, and often police increase patrols near schools on the weekends

Do you have a drug-testing program?

Listen/look for: drug-testing programs are under increased scrutiny by the courts; debating if testing of all students, athletes, band members, or teachers for drugs is legal has led some districts to institute voluntary drug-testing programs

What happens if a child is caught with drugs?

Listen/look for: normally a student found with illegal drugs in his possession is suspended from school, possibly pending an expulsion hearing before the school board; additionally, suspect students are reported to the police for possible legal action

What is DARE?

Listen/look for: Drug Awareness Resistance Education

POLICE AND THE SCHOOL

The involvement of police in schools was once a rare occurrence. Today, more and more schools are finding themselves working closely with police authorities because of the focus on drugs, violence, and school safety. In some districts police are actually called to the school to take into custody students that in the past were handled by school principals. In a growing number of schools, students violating dress codes, disrupting the educational process, or fighting are being taken to jail rather than being assigned traditional detention. Regardless of the degree of local tolerance for misbehavior at school, police and school officials have discovered that they must use a team approach in meeting the many challenges that face schools.

What Is the Relationship between the School and the Police?

One extremely helpful agreement between police and the school officials is a memorandum of understanding (MOU), an important written document in the coordination of emergency efforts during a crisis. This agreement between local police, fire, and emergency management personnel and the school district must be undertaken as a part of crisis preparedness. In most cases several meetings take place between the agencies to develop a unified plan for reacting to emergencies in the schools. It usually contains sections related to protocols of agencies involved in school incidents, release of information, scope of the school participation, compliance with state and federal regulations, and when and if legal authorities are to be called to the school.

One of its primary purposes is to outline the responsibilities of each agency before an emergency occurs. While the existence of an MOU is critical, the initial reaction of the principal in the building, before the police arrive, is vital to successful emergency response.

Questions to Consider

Does the school have a procedural agreement, such as an MOU, with local police on emergency procedures?
Listen/look for: most schools have agreements with local police and fire departments; in emergency situations, response personnel must have a knowledge of the building site in order to perform their valuable function

What police agency has jurisdiction in school-related matters?
Listen/look for: every school lies within some police jurisdiction; while some urban or suburban schools may have only one police agency with jurisdiction, some larger rural schools may have several agencies up to and including the state police

Can a Child Be Arrested while at School?

Students believed to have violated a legally enacted statute may be questioned and arrested while at school by police authorities. More and more schools are relying on police to remove disruptive students. Sometimes, depending on the age of the student, parents may be contacted by police. However, parents must realize that when it is a police matter, the legal authorities, and not the school, control the situation.

Questions to Consider

Can a child be searched at school?
Listen/look for: many school officials use reasonable suspicion regarding the need to search a student; if a school official has a reason to sus-

pect that a student may have a dangerous weapon or possess material that may be harmful to the student or to others, the principal may choose to search the student; many times parents are called to the school and asked to participate in the inquiry

Don't parents have to be called before police question their child?
Listen/look for: often police will contact parents of minors, but police will not wait to ask preliminary questions of suspects if a possible crime has been committed

Can a Student's Car Be Searched?

Once again, violation of law can result in police action including frisk searches, locker searches, and searches of automobiles. School authorities may, under some circumstances, search a student's locker, purse, or person. In emergency situations, searches may be conducted for the safety of the school population. Local school officials may have specific policies relevant to such searches. Normally if a police officer clearly sees an illegal item in an automobile, he has the right to search that vehicle without a warrant (local police may have alternative and more detailed information related to automobile searches).

Questions to Consider

Who calls the police?
Listen/look for: normally the school principal, secretary, or security officer calls police; in the event of an emergency many schools have protocols that outline who is to contact police agencies

Under what circumstances would a student's car be searched at school?
Listen/look for: a student's car may be searched if an illegal item is clearly seen through the window; students may be asked to voluntarily open their car for inspection

Will the parents be called to be present when their child's car is searched on school property?
Listen/look for: in most cases student cars are searched without parent involvement; once an illegal item is found, parents are called at once

When Are Police Called to the School?

Police are called to the school whenever a criminal act is committed or thought to have been committed. School principals contact police agencies when there is a threat to the school or to members of the school community that is beyond the ability of the school authorities to handle or when the incident falls under the memorandum of understanding. Incidents such as bomb threats, weapon possession, unlawful entry, drug issues, or events involving any illegal act mandate contact with the police. Police are usually not called to the school in response to matters of stealing, minor fighting, harassment, or other routine school matters because principals typically deal with violations of basic school rules. When police are called to the school grounds, they enter the situation as legal authorities with the ability to arrest and take into custody. The matter then becomes a police matter, and the school is only a reporting agency.

Questions to Consider

Are police called to the school when a fight is reported?
Listen/look for: calling police to the school in response to an altercation is a decision made by the building principal; unless the fight involves large numbers of students or an actual assault has taken place, police are not normally called to the school; school rules typically outline when police are to be called

Are police called when weapons are suspected in the building?
Listen/look for: most local police departments recommend that they be called whenever there is a suspected weapon in the school building or on school property; police would prefer to respond to the school and find no weapon than not be called and as a result someone is injured by a weapon

Can a Child's Locker Be Searched?

Students are assigned lockers to be used for the temporary storage of school-related materials. As such, they remain the property of the school. In most schools, students are reminded yearly that the lockers are school property and subject to searches. As evidence of school ownership, locks are assigned with master keys stored in the office. Additionally, students need to be informed that drug-sniffing dogs, weapon-sniffing dogs, and police personnel can search school lockers if there is probable cause.

To avoid the appearance of discrimination, school officials typically search in specific ways. All lockers can be searched, a randomly selected bank of lockers may be searched, or every tenth locker can be searched. Furthermore, if a school official has reason to believe (reasonable suspicion) that a locker contains illegal or dangerous material, it may be inspected.

Questions to Consider

Do the police need a warrant to search a child's locker?
Listen/look for: often police do need a warrant to search a specific locker for a specific item; when drug dogs discover evidence of possible drugs in a locker, it is often the school official that actually opens the locker for the police

How do parents know that drugs or a weapon was not planted in their child's locker?
Listen/look for: students are given private lock combinations to protect the contents of their lockers; students should not share their combinations with others; when school officials search a locker they normally have witnesses that verify what is found; some schools also videotape locker searches to eliminate accusations of a planted item

Can personal articles be taken out of a child's locker during a search?
Listen/look for: local laws may regulate seizure of items; illegal items or items inappropriate for school use can often be confiscated

Who is authorized to search a child's locker?
Listen/look for: depending on the circumstances, the school principal or other adult acting for the school or the police can open a child's locker for just cause

Under what circumstances would the principal open a student's locker?
Listen/look for: principals typically would open a student's locker if they feel the locker contains an item or substance inappropriate for school (drugs, weapons, drug paraphernalia, stolen property)

Can a Child Be Searched?

Some schools have instituted the searching of students to a greater extent than others. Basically, school officials have the right to request a student to empty his or her pockets and remain in a supervised placement until police or parents arrive. In the event that an illegal item or substance is found, the school authorities will hold it and keep it under lock and key until the police arrive. Police, on the other hand, can and will search a student if they have "probable cause." This means the police have reason to believe that there has been a probable violation of the law and that the subject warrants close scrutiny. School officials, on the other hand, may not be held to as strict an interpretation if there is reasonable suspicion that school policy has been violated or a dangerous situation exists. Normally, reasonable suspicion implies that the school employee has a compelling reason to believe that a violation has been committed.

Questions to Consider

Do you have a "zero tolerance" policy?
Listen/look for: many educators feel that schools have operated on a "zero tolerance" basis for years in as much as they have never "tolerated" drugs or weapons in schools; in many schools students found with drugs or weapons are almost always referred to the school board for possible expulsion

What does it mean?
Listen/look for: the commonly accepted definition of a zero tolerance policy is that students found with a weapon in their possession will automatically be expelled from school; in actuality, most states permit some discretion on the part of the school superintendent to deal on a case-by-case basis

Can a child's person be searched by a school official?
Listen/look for: as stated earlier, school authorities have the right to search a child's locker and ask a student to empty purses and pockets; individual state laws may regulate the length a school employee can go in searching students

Who is authorized to conduct a body search of a child?
Listen/look for: in most schools intrusive body searches are not permitted

Are police called to search students?
Listen/look for: in some cases police may be called to conduct a lawful search of a student if he or she is considered to be in possession of a dangerous weapon or drugs

Will the parents be called to be present when their child is searched?
Listen/look for: school officials almost always attempt to contact parents when a child is involved in a serious incident; police often contact parents but will not wait for parental consent if they conclude that there is a dangerous situation

Doesn't the search violate a child's right to privacy?
Listen/look for: children have the right to bring lawful items to school; children do not have a constitutional right to possess items that are illegal or constitute a threat to others

Can a teacher search a child when looking for missing money in her class?
Listen/look for: in cases of theft, the school principal should be contacted, parents should be contacted, and students should be sequestered in a room under supervision; many educators agree that the possible legal issues that can result from searching all of the students make it ill-advised

What if parents do not give permission for their child to be searched without their presence?
Listen/look for: police will search any person considered to be violating the law without parental permission; school officials often keep the child under surveillance and wait until the parent arrives to search the student; local policies regulate the procedures normally followed

What happens if a child accidentally has a knife in his pocket?
Listen/look for: under a strict zero tolerance policy, some school districts have expelled students for the possession of small knives; many superintendents will consider extenuating circumstances when rendering a decision related to punishment for violations of the weapons policy

CHAPTER 2

The Parent

COMMUNICATION WITH THE SCHOOL

Today's principals must make every effort to open lines of communication, not only with parents but also with all members of the school community. Each year, more and more taxpayers no longer have children enrolled in school, and the need exists to inform and educate parents of former students as well as nonparents. Modern principals use a variety of tools to correspond with their constituents. Newsletters, handbooks, television presentations, speeches to community organizations, and articles in local newspapers are only a few of the many approaches that are utilized. Principals can no longer wait for the media representative to come to the school looking for a story. They must be proactive in highlighting the positive happenings in the school.

Addressing letters and notices to the school is completed in the normal manner. Usually stating the teacher's name and room number is enough when the notice is sent to school with a child. If the letter is being mailed to the school, the proper name, room number, and school address is appropriate. The heading of the letter should begin by indicating the teacher's name, followed by the body of the note, and concluding with the signature and phone number of the parent. Be certain to include all needed information such as time, place, and dates to clarify the message.

Questions to Consider

What is the proper way to address a note to school?
Listen/look for: ordinarily notes to school should be addressed to a specific person or department within the school; if sent to school with a student, it is helpful if the child's name is on the outside of the note (in the event it is misplaced)

What if the parent does not know the name of the person she wants to contact?
Listen/look for: if the name of the specific person is unknown, stating the department or general title ("To the teacher of Billy Jones") is appropriate

How long do parents have to wait for a reply to their letter?
Listen/look for: unless the subject is time sensitive, a response should be received within a few days

What Should Parents Say When They Call the School?

Calling the school is similar to calling any professional organization. Knowing exactly whom you wish to talk to, thinking through the reason for your call, and getting to the point make calls beneficial to the caller and timely for the school. State your name, the reason for the call, whom you wish to speak to, and if that person is unavailable, when you can be reached. Don't forget to give your phone number.

Questions to Consider

Who will answer the phone at school?
Listen/look for: schools have secretaries or receptionists who answer incoming phone calls

What time during the day can a parent talk to teachers?
Listen/look for: every school district has differing times that teachers are available to receive phone calls; it is recommended that parents call the school and leave a message for a teacher to return the call; early in the morning, before school starts, during the teacher's planning period, during lunch, or immediately after school are possible times teachers can return phone calls

Can a parent call and talk to the principal if she has a private matter to discuss?

Listen/look for: yes, principals welcome parental contact to help with any problem that could affect a child's education; if the principal is not available when called, he will return the call as soon as possible

Can a parent talk directly to the guidance teacher if she has a private matter to discuss?

Listen/look for: yes, guidance personnel are available to discuss issues related to students

Will the parent and teacher conversations be kept in strict confidence?

Listen/look for: yes, guidance personnel keep information from parents confidential unless it poses a threat or danger to other students or the school population

Will the secretary look up information for a parent?

Listen/look for: parents calling the school must be aware that the person receiving the phone call does not know the true identity of the person on the other end of the line; confidential information will often not be given over the phone

What if the parent does not know his child's teacher's name?

Listen/look for: typically the secretary will take the caller's name and phone number and, after looking up the teacher's name, give her the message

Can a parent talk to the nurse?

Listen/look for: the school nurse is usually available to talk to parents, but remember that the nurse does not know the true identity of the caller; no medical information will be given over the phone

Can a parent call the school and have his child excused early?

Listen/look for: most schools operate on the "signed note" method of excusing a student early; in addition, many schools require parents to come to the office and identify themselves before picking up their child

Can a parent call the school and report her child off of school for the day?
Listen/look for: yes, most schools accept a call from a parent reporting a student absent, but a signed excuse note is usually required before the absence is counted as legal; once again, the school does not know the validity of the caller

Are Report Cards Useful?

Report cards are one approach to notifying parents of the progress of their child in academic areas. As such, they can be very useful to parents in ascertaining the effort being put forth by the child and areas where additional help and work on the student's part are needed. Some report cards allow space for teacher comments. If this is true of a child's report card, the parent should read the comment carefully and if necessary call the teacher to clarify the statement. While report cards are valuable tools for reporting progress, a personal conference with the teacher should be arranged if problems exist.

Questions to Consider

What is the school's grading policy?
Listen/look for: grading policies differ across school districts; school boards approve grading policies and administrators and teachers administer the policy in their school

What use are report cards?
Listen/look for: report cards are used to communicate the academic progress of children in school

When are report cards sent home?
Listen/look for: report cards may be sent home every six or nine weeks; some districts may have reporting periods of differing time frames

What if a parent chooses not to sign a child's report card?
Listen/look for: in most school districts signing a report card indicates that the parent has had the opportunity to read the report; in some schools failure to sign the report card may result in a phone call from the school to inquire if it has been seen

Aren't narrative comments better than As, Bs, and Cs on a report card?
Listen/look for: many educators prefer a narrative reporting system because it tends to provide more specific information related to student progress; some schools use an A, B, C system and write comments to accompany the letter grades; still other schools use O (outstanding), S (satisfactory), N (needs improvement), or some other form of notification of student growth

What if a parent wants more information than the report provides?
Listen/look for: report cards are only a summary of work completed; parents wishing more detailed information concerning their child's progress should request a parent–teacher conference

Does a child's attendance affect his grades?
Listen/look for: in most districts, attendance is not counted against grades, but all principals and teachers feel that good attendance is important and strive to encourage students to attend on a regular basis; they encourage parents to take their vacations when school is not in session; attendance may be considered when students are having a problem in school because being present in class is necessary for learning to take place

How Do Parents Know the Grades Are Given Fairly?

In the vast majority of cases, teachers are involved in the education of children because of an innate desire to help children. Few professional educators spend the many required years in college and work for what some might consider lower than adequate pay in order to treat children unfairly. Teachers attempt to instill in their students the qualities of trust and the need to eliminate discrimination. As such, teachers approach grading tests and papers as an opportunity to reinforce concepts learned or as a means to communicate the need for the student to relearn or study harder in the future.

In cases where a parent truly feels that a grade has been given erroneously or by mistake, the teacher should be contacted for clarification. In most cases the teacher will have a legitimate reason for the grade given.

Questions to Consider

Why do some children get all the good grades and some always get Fs?

Listen/look for: there are many reasons why some students receive failing grades; poor study habits, learning disabilities, attention deficit disorders, or inattention may result in poor grades

Does the principal ever look at a teacher's test to see if it is fair?

Listen/look for: often principals will ask teachers to submit their tests for review; test construction is not necessarily easy, and some teachers may need assistance learning how to create a reliable test

If a parent has a confrontation with a teacher, will her child's grades suffer?

Listen/look for: teachers are never permitted to punish students through grades; confrontations with parents should be considered disagreements between adults only; a child's grades should reflect his performance on assigned schoolwork

What does a child's academic grades have to do with his participating on a sports team?

Listen/look for: many secondary schools have eligibility lists that require students to maintain a certain grade average to participate in a sport; it is often felt that a student should be academically worthy to represent his school on the athletic field

Aren't some students "teacher's pets"?

Listen/look for: some teachers have students that they depend on to respond to questions, run notes to the office, help clean up the room, and communicate with them in a respectful manner; these students may be viewed as "teacher's pets"

Why are some grades subjective?

Listen/look for: many questions on tests require a narrative answer or essay response; these types of questions are judged with a degree of subjectivity because there are various elements involved in correctly answering the questions

Can a parent see all of his child's grades to determine if they are correct?

Listen/look for: yes, teachers are required to show parents their child's grades; confidentiality requires that no other student's grades may be shared

Can a teacher punish a child for poor behavior by dropping his grade?

Listen/look for: in some schools grades are given for conduct in class; often in kindergarten or first grade some indication is recorded on report cards showing a child's behavior and cooperation; lowering of grades should not be used as punishment

Will the teacher explain the grades on the report card?

Listen/look for: while grades are usually explained on the report card, teachers will clarify the meaning and source of grades

What if the teacher makes a mistake on the report card?

Listen/look for: if a teacher makes a mistake and marks a grade incorrectly on the report card, she can correct the mistake and change the grade on the student's permanent file

Is the report card part of a child's permanent record?

Listen/look for: yes, grades earned in school become part of a student's permanent educational record; in many districts grades earned at the elementary level are kept until high school, where grades nine through twelve are considered more relevant for meeting graduation requirements

Does the PTA Send Notices Home?

Most Parent Teacher Associations (PTA) or Parent Teacher Organizations (PTO) send home information of interest to parents. At the elementary level, where such organizations are often very active, monthly newsletters, notices of upcoming events, and sheets announcing fundraising attempts are frequently used. Care must be taken to remind children to bring home notices given to them at school. Too often, children lose notices, resulting in missed opportunities to be fully involved in school activities.

At the secondary level, the PTA and PTO also send home information. Notices of open houses, organizational meetings, and issues of interest are either sent home or mailed.

Questions to Consider

Does the local PTA or PTO send home notices?
Listen/look for: the PTA and other parent organizations normally send notices home at the elementary level; as students move into higher grade levels, communications are often conveyed to parents via school district notices and media announcements

If parents have a question about the PTA, whom do they contact?
Listen/look for: principals are happy to provide the names and phone numbers of officers in the parents' organization

How active is your PTA?
Listen/look for: the activity of the PTA in schools depends on the involvement of the parents in the school; normally elementary schools are most active, and as students get older they are less inclined to want their parents involved in school; parents are encouraged to join the PTA

Can parents attend the next PTA meeting?
Listen/look for: some PTAs hold executive meetings monthly and general membership meetings a few times a year; local PTA officers can provide the dates appropriate for general members to attend

How often does the PTA hold its general meetings?
Listen/look for: every school is different, but general membership meetings are commonly held three or four times a year

What services does the PTA provide for the students?
Listen/look for: typically, PTAs help provide extra funds and opportunities for students such as field trips, special assemblies, supplemental supplies for the classroom, equipment to enrich instruction, and assistance at school dances and parties

Can a parent write an article for the PTA newsletter?
Listen/look for: often PTA editors welcome contributions from members as long as the article is unbiased and does not cast a negative light on the work of the PTA

Does the principal see the PTA notices before they go home?
Listen/look for: principals should review every notice that leaves the school including the PTA newsletter; verification of information avoids confusion

How Important Is Communication between the Teacher and the Parent?

Personal contact with the schoolteacher is very important. If school personnel do not communicate to the degree that parents feel is needed, the parents must take the initiative to contact the school for current information about their child.

Questions to Consider

Will the school ever call parents with good news?
Listen/look for: many principals and teachers delight in calling parents with good news about their children; outstanding effort, above average grades, recognition as student of the week, and special acknowledgment for work well done should be communicated to parents

Will teachers ever call parents regarding their child?
Listen/look for: many principals request teachers to call home when there is a minor problem concerning a child; teachers recognize that working with parents to solve a small problem may help avoid an escalation of the problem

How will parents know if an important letter is being sent home with a child?
Listen/look for: elementary schools routinely send home notices on a specific day of the week (perhaps Fridays); letters of a very important nature are often mailed home; it is recommended that elementary parents look in their child's book bag for notices sent home

Does the principal ever meet with groups of parents to discuss concerns?
Listen/look for: principals often hold meetings with individuals and groups concerning specific issues; a change in a class schedule, a change in a child's teacher, review of field trip guidelines, committees

of parents related to school projects, and alterations in bus routes are a few of the reasons principals may schedule meetings with parents

Are meetings ever held in the evening for parents when they are off work?
Listen/look for: principals are aware that most parents work during the course of the school day; often meetings are arranged for early evening to accommodate parents

Will the principal meet with parents if they have a concern?
Listen/look for: public school principals should be available to meet with a parent at any reasonable time; adequate notice may be necessary to avoid conflicts, but as educational leaders, principals are eager to meet with and discuss concerns related to a child's education

How Can a Parent Learn about the School Curriculum?

Many school districts have directors or supervisors of curriculum. These individuals are responsible for monitoring, advancing, and communicating the board's approved school curriculum. Additionally, the school principal should be well versed in the substance of the various curriculum areas within his or her school. Teachers, as well, are knowledgeable about the courses they teach and the value of the curriculum that forms the basis of their instructional day.

Questions to Consider

If something changes in the curriculum, will parents be told?
Listen/look for: notices in local papers or on local television news programs, school board minutes, and notices sent home from the school; PTA groups normally keep a watchful eye on the curriculum within a district and notify parents of any proposed changes

If a new program is going to be implemented, will parents be notified?
Listen/look for: when new programs are proposed for implementation, most schools inform parents of the possibility and request input into the decision; in many districts informational meetings are held before pro-

grams such as drug testing, sex education, and teen pregnancy are instituted

If a child is gifted, do you have a program to accommodate his needs?

Listen/look for: some schools have specific programs designed to meet the needs of talented and gifted children; some schools have accelerated classes, advanced placement classes, and pull-out gifted programs designed to challenge students with higher than normal intelligence

Can a parent borrow a text to review?

Listen/look for: typically schools have very few extra textbooks, but parents with specific concerns related to a textbook in use can usually arrange to borrow a book for a short period of time

Can a child use a tape recorder while a teacher is teaching?

Listen/look for: note taking is an important skill to acquire in school; schools will normally permit tape recording of a teacher's lecture if permission is requested and the teacher is fully aware of the reason and times of the recordings; some teacher's contracts may have restrictions on tape recording a teacher's presentation

Can a parent borrow the curriculum guide to review?

Listen/look for: guides are normally available for parental review either at the school site or at the district office

Can a parent read the teacher's lesson plans?

Listen/look for: teacher lesson plans are only plans, and as such they are designed to help the teacher organize her instruction; lesson plans reveal nothing related to the skill of the teacher or her ability to teach effectively; most schools would see little value in parents reading a teacher's lesson plans

Can a parent attend district curriculum meetings?

Listen/look for: school board curriculum meetings are generally open to the public; committee meetings of teachers in the process of developing curricular areas are most often formative in nature and are open to educators only

Does the school board ever discuss curriculum?

Listen/look for: yes, school boards often discuss curricular areas as part of their regular board meetings; review of new programs, questions related to contents of current programs, recent research concerning proposed curriculum, and questions from the public relative to course content may be discussed by the school board in open sessions

If parents disagree with the new sex education curriculum, can their child be exempt?

Listen/look for: some schools permit alternative courses in lieu of required courses for individual students with conflicting religious beliefs; elective courses at the high school level permit students to choose classes that meet their interests

Can parents suggest ideas related to the curriculum to the school board?

Listen/look for: yes, parents are always welcome at most school board meetings; suggestions and ideas related to improved instruction are invited as long as they are presented in an organized, constructive manner

How Can Parents Learn about New Programs?

When a district is considering a new program, curriculum, or course, district leaders should be proactive in informing the public early in the process. Educators have found that the involvement of shareholders (parents, students, teachers, and so on) in the process of any new endeavor is critical to its success. Communication via the written word, public meetings, and individual meetings with school representatives help promote and explain new approaches being considered.

Questions to Consider

Can a parent read the research in support of a proposed new program?

Listen/look for: normally central office curriculum directors have extensive research related to proposed new programs; parents are welcome to borrow and read any research of interest

How does a parent know what is being offered to his child for the next school year?
Listen/look for: course outlines are usually available in the spring of the year

Do teachers put assignments on the Internet?
Listen/look for: some school districts have the capacity to provide teacher's assignments on a web page; individual teachers may or may not wish to provide assignments because taking notes and recording assignments is part of developing good study habits

How does a parent find out about summer school?
Listen/look for: look for notices posted on school bulletin boards, look for PTA notices, or contact the school principal

How Do Parents Learn about the School Rules?

Most schools today publish and issue both a parent handbook and a student handbook. Both of these publications normally outline rules and regulations in the school.

Parents wishing to know more about the school rules and district school board regulations and policies can consult the central administrative office to obtain (or at least read) the district policy handbook. Every policy to be administered in the schools must be passed by the school board. Individual school principals may initiate school rules that further delineate, clarify, and expound upon district policies.

Questions to Consider

Can a parent have a copy of the school rules?
Listen/look for: customarily school rules are outlined in the student handbook and/or parent handbook; specific information can be obtained from the school district policy handbook

Does the school have a student handbook?
Listen/look for: the majority of schools have student handbooks to clarify student rights and responsibilities

Who makes the school rules?
Listen/look for: groups of district educators usually develop school rules, which are then approved by the school board

How much physical force can teachers use with students?
Listen/look for: teachers as a rule have the right to protect themselves and the safety of others in the course of their work; some teachers are trained in passive restraint

What kinds of punishment can be assigned?
Listen/look for: a variety of punishments are assigned depending on the violation; time-outs, apologies, detentions, suspensions, and expulsions are examples of consequences assigned

Do school rules permit corporal punishment?
Listen/look for: most schools have eliminated the use of corporal punishment

Are teachers allowed to touch a child?
Listen/look for: the prudent teacher knows the dangers of touching a student; many feel that a pat on the back for work well done and the redirecting of a student by touching him on the arm are permissible; parents need to be reminded that it is very difficult for a kindergarten teacher to go through a day of teaching without drying a few tears, receiving hugs, or consoling a child; part of teaching is compassion and sensitivity to the needs of students

Are students assigned written assignments for punishment?
Listen/look for: many teachers and principals dislike assignments of written work as punishment; it is perceived that using written work as punishment sends a message that writing is a punishment

Will a child be embarrassed in front of others?
Listen/look for: embarrassment in front of others is a poor approach; many teachers have found that embarrassment causes resentment and increased disrespect, and it may result in disrespect from other students

What if a child does not understand the rules?
Listen/look for: older children should ask for clarification of rules; younger students should have the rules clearly explained to them in a simple, easily understood way

Does the school have any authority over a child on his way to and from school?
Listen/look for: schools (acting in loco parentis) often have authority over students going to and from school; rules are made for conduct on the buses, and misbehavior by students while walking home usually results in school consequences; local laws and district regulations may clarify the jurisdiction of schools

How Can Parents Meet the Teacher?

Teachers are usually eager to meet parents. They feel that the success of any student's educational experience depends on a team effort between the school and the home. As the child's first teachers, the parents' involvement is critical. Many schools hold open houses in the early part of the year, providing parents the opportunity to meet their child's teachers. PTA meetings may be an avenue to meet teachers and discuss issues of school concern. Individual programs are typically offered at the elementary level such as Parents' Day, Grandparents' Day, Christmas concerts, and special classroom festivities.

Questions to Consider

Can a parent come to school before the school year begins to meet the teacher?
Listen/look for: many times teachers are not in the building until the last few days before school resumes for the year; unless there is a special, compelling reason to meet with a child's new teacher, it is usually best to wait until the teacher gets to know the child; that does not mean that a parent with special concerns should not meet with the school principal before school starts; most schools have orientation programs for parents of students new to the school, often the week before school starts

When is the school open house being held?
Listen/look for: open houses are usually held about the first or second month of school so that teachers are familiar with students they are teaching; that does not mean that a parent with a concern should wait until the open house to contact the teacher

Can parents call the teacher at school to discuss their child?
Listen/look for: yes, teachers appreciate a call from parents to discuss student concerns; remember that a teacher is engaged in teaching most of the day and may not be readily available when you first call

Can parents meet with their child's teacher monthly or quarterly?
Listen/look for: teachers, like many professionals, are very busy people; parents that have a specific concern or problem related to their child are certainly welcome to meet with their child's teacher periodically; setting up monthly or quarterly meetings in anticipation of a problem is usually not necessary or recommended

PARENT EXPECTATIONS

What Can a Parent Do, Right Now, to Help His Child in School?

Parents have an important role to play in a child's education. Parents that support school rules, encourage completion of assignments, participate in school activities, and support parent groups such as the PTA help their child. Additionally, serving as a role model by reading, taking academics seriously, and cooperating with school officials motivates students to emulate their parents and enhances learning.

Questions to Consider

Can you help parents control their child?
Listen/look for: guidance counselors typically can attempt to help parents address some behavioral problems; in many cases they have resources available that they can recommend if the concerns are serious

Can you help parents get their child to school on time?
Listen/look for: it is the parents' responsibility to see that students arrive at school on time; certainly school attendance officers can meet with students and stress the importance of regular and timely attendance, but it is the parents' responsibility

Can you help parents get their child to dress appropriately?
Listen/look for: as long as the student does not violate the school's student dress code, the school cannot become involved in matters related to student dress

Can you help parents make their child behave?
Listen/look for: most guidance counselors and student support teams are willing to share ideas and strategies that may improve student behavior; however, parents need to be reminded that the thrust of the school is behavior as it relates to schoolwork and educational success

Can you help parents make their child do his homework?
Listen/look for: school officials may be able to offer ideas to help address a student's unwillingness to complete homework; consequences may be applied at school, and parents should consider implementing consequences at home for a student's refusal to do schoolwork

Can you make a child wear her glasses in school?
Listen/look for: if parents let the school know that a child is supposed to wear her glasses at all times, the teacher can remind the child; if a student refuses to bring her glasses to school, there is little that the school can do

What Is a Child Permitted to Do in School?

Schools have rules. These rules are in place for the overall safety and successful operation of the school program. Normally, such rules are based on an identified need, and this need should be known to students and understood by parents. While every school has specific rules and regulations, they generally represent well thought out, acceptable approaches to meeting a common concern in the school environment.

Parents should read the student or parent handbook and then, if a need for clarity exists, consult the school principal. When a rule seems unfair or unreasonable, after discussing it with the principal, consultation with district office representatives may be needed.

Questions to Consider

Can a child bring a snack to school for midmorning?

Listen/look for: sometimes midmorning snacks are permitted in kindergarten; after kindergarten students are expected to come to school having had a healthy breakfast, eat a sustaining lunch, and wait until they reach home for afternoon snacks

Can the students in a classroom buy a gift for the teacher?

Listen/look for: many schools do not recommend that students contribute money toward a present for a teacher; many times in the past, one or two students have ended up paying most of the cost for the present because some members of the class did not bring in their money; some schools suggest that if parents wish to buy small gifts for a teacher it be on an individual basis

Can a child stay inside for recess?

Listen/look for: recess in most elementary schools is an important outlet for students' pent up energy; in many schools all students are expected to go out for recess; if there is a temporary health-related problem, parents should write a note to the teacher requesting that their child be permitted to stay inside that day for recess

Can a child be excused from physical education for a week?

Listen/look for: if health-related problems exist, most schools will excuse students from physical education classes for a specific period of time; some schools require a doctor's excuse before excusing a student from gym class

Can a child bring a cell phone to school?

Listen/look for: the possession of a cell phone in school is normally regulated by the students' rights and responsibilities guidelines; some schools allow cell phones, but they must be turned off during the school day; other schools prohibit student cell phones altogether

Why can't a child wear what she wants to school?

Listen/look for: some schools have student dress codes that disallow some types of clothing in school; usually common sense and decency dictate the prohibition of shirts with objectionable language and symbols, overly tight or short clothing, and attire that would cause a disruption of the educational process; students need to be reminded that they are in school to learn, not to cause havoc and a commotion

Why is a student dress code necessary?

Listen/look for: many school officials believe that a uniform dress code reduces gang-related clothing in the school; some school principals feel that a dress code helps avoid the clothing discrepancy between students of various income levels; unfortunately, some parents do not display common sense in relation to student dress

If a parent selects and buys a sweatshirt or dress, why can't a child wear it?

Listen/look for: good taste and commonly accepted apparel are appropriate for school wear; school officials will not tolerate clothing with gang slogans, with obscene language, or that interferes with the educational process; clothing of inappropriate length or suggestive in nature may be banned, as well as halter tops, tank tops, bare midriffs, fish nets, and excessively tight jeans

Can a child be excused from an assembly if the noise upsets him?

Listen/look for: students that have a negative reaction to loud noises or other conditions found in some assemblies may be excused if the parent notifies the school of the problem

Can a Parent Believe What Other Parents Say about the School?

Every parent has an impression of his or her child's school. In some cases it may be colored by a poor experience resulting in a negative feeling about the school. However, in most cases, parents feel good about their child's school and will candidly share their experiences and perceptions about teachers, the school environment, and the principal. When negative perceptions are encountered, it is wise to seek additional parent input. This will help the inquiring parent gain a more realistic picture of the school. When the overall perception of the school is positive, the parent can normally rest assured that the school is working well. In cases where the overall view of the school is poor or negative, the inquiring parent should visit the school, meet with the principal, talk with the teachers, and form his or her own unbiased perception.

Questions to Consider

Do all parents like the school?
Listen/look for: individual parents may have positive or negative feelings about the school; at times some parents may disagree with school policies or procedures and develop a disapproving impression of the school; it is usually best to discuss the impressions of the school with several different parents before forming an impression; of course, the best way to form a personal impression of the school and its policies is to work with the school officials and develop an individual perception

With whom can a parent talk and really learn about the school?
Listen/look for: parents that attend school programs, talk with members of the PTA, and discuss school issues with neighbors often gain realistic impressions of the school

What does the principal think parents would say about the school?
Listen/look for: principals would hope that parents would say the school is a safe, positive place for students to be, a rich learning environment that provides a high-quality educational opportunity

Will the PTA president talk about the school honestly?
Listen/look for: yes, PTA officers often work very closely with the school and know both its positive points and negative points

Why would a parent tell lies about the school?
Listen/look for: some parents that have experienced conflict with school officials may have developed a negative perception of the school and express dissatisfaction with school performance

Have other parents disagreed with the policies of the school?
Listen/look for: it is not unusual for almost every school policy to have detractors and individuals with objections to its application; principals often hear complaints about some rules, particularly when a parent's child has faced the consequences of violating the rule

Is it true that some teachers do not get along in school?
Listen/look for: schools are much like families, and as such, members occasionally experience disagreements; teachers are professionals and are

expected to conduct themselves as mature adults; when differences arise, all staff members involved are to resolve the matter in an adult manner

Don't public schools have more disciplinary problems than do private schools?
Listen/look for: schools consist of children, and regardless of the type of school, disciplinary problems exist; some private schools can be more selective of the students they enroll, while public schools must admit all students within their attendance area; every school has its share of disciplinary problems

What Can a Parent Reasonably Expect from a Public School?

Parents of children attending public schools should insist that certain conditions be in place for the safety and educational utilization of their children. While most schools demonstrate the majority of these qualities, a wise parent will monitor and assess the degree to which individual schools are meeting their expectations.

Generally speaking, a parent should expect the following from a public school:

- A safe school—a safe and secure environment is crucial to learning.
- A caring staff—a concerned and compassionate staff is necessary.
- A concerned principal—a responsible and proactive principal is required.
- A calm environment—a pleasant, quiet workspace is advantageous to learning.
- A clean building—a health-conscious and well-maintained building is needed.
- An enriching curriculum—a curriculum based on currency and relevance is vital.
- Respect for every child—acceptance and respect for all children are required.
- Reasonable rules—well-developed, clearly explained rules add consistency.
- A fair discipline policy—consistent, fair, and reasonable rules provide structure.

- Fair implementation of discipline—unbiased, just application of rules is vital.
- Open communication—two-way communication avoids misunderstandings.
- Freedom from drugs—attempts must be made to protect students from the influence of drugs.
- Well-developed policies—well-developed, clearly written district policies promote compliance.
- Help when needed—a means to assist the underachiever, the special needs child, and the child experiencing difficulties that interfere with learning is a requirement.
- Reasonable class size—a reasonable class size permits an acceptable teacher–student ratio.
- Integration of technology—modernized use of technology benefits students.
- Open fiscal responsibility—clarity of understanding and accountability of funds are necessary.
- An approachable principal and staff—the principal and staff must welcome parents' help.
- Reasonable assignments—policies must be implemented that enhance classwork at home.
- Comfortable surroundings—a pleasant, calm, and enjoyable environment enhances learning.

Often parents have questions related to the expectations of schools and the allowable behaviors related to school life. The issue of school reform is currently an area of interest to parents.

Questions to Consider

What is school reform all about?
Listen/look for: over the years many approaches have been taken to address school reform; some individuals feel that the public schools should be better; various alternatives have been proposed, including charter schools; many feel giving parents a choice will create competition and public schools will improve; while there is little doubt that schools can always be better, many educators believe they are delivering a quality education, considering the number and wide range of abilities they must teach

Are charter schools better than public schools?
Listen/look for: the debate goes on; advocates of charter schools feel they must provide a good education or they will go out of business; public school educators see the charter school movement as a drain on funding for public education; most principals welcome the opportunity to discuss charter schools

Aren't charter schools really private schools?
Listen/look for: in most states, charter schools are considered public schools; many private schools often have a religious base

Must parents allow their child to participate in fund-raising?
Listen/look for: some schools permit parents to make a monetary contribution rather than have their child participate in fund-raising; a child does not have to go door to door

Should parents keep a child home for another year or send him to kindergarten?
Listen/look for: many educators feel that another year at home with a parent is appropriate if the parent provides an enriched experience of reading and visits to cultural activities; however, if a child is going to spend his time watching television and playing video games, he is better off enrolled in a kindergarten class

How Important Are Student Records?

Student records are important in the operation of schools. Any history of drug use or weapon violations must be maintained in a student's permanent record to permit future disciplinary action if the behavior is repeated. At the same time, parents are concerned about the availability of student records to the casual viewer. Strict rules should be in place to guard against unauthorized and unnecessary review of student records.

Questions to Consider

Does a discipline problem remain in a child's permanent record?
Listen/look for: usually the records of minor discipline problems remain in a child's file for the current year only; generally school records

are further purged when a child moves to the next level of schooling (elementary, middle/junior high, high school); records of drug use, weapon possession, and other serious violations remain in a student's file until he or she graduates

Is a child's health problem part of his permanent school record?
Listen/look for: often health problems are kept as part of a student file only as long as the problem exists and the school needs the information

Can a parent remove a child's special placement designation from her school records?
Listen/look for: school records are legal documents that substantiate a child's performance in school; as such, a special placement has bearing on the grades she has received

What school information is sent to potential employers?
Listen/look for: after graduation, a graduate's final grade point average, address, and classes attended may customarily be sent to potential employers when authorized by the student

Can police see a child's school record?
Listen/look for: typically police need a warrant to view a student's personal file

Will a student be labeled when employers read his school file?
Listen/look for: if a student has poor grades he may not be chosen for a position

What student records are sent from the elementary school to the middle school?
Listen/look for: elementary records are usually purged between elementary and middle school; transcripts, IEPs, standardized test results, copies of report cards, health-related matters, and serious violations of school rules may be forwarded

What student records are sent from the middle school to the high school?
Listen/look for: middle school records are usually purged between middle and high school; transcripts, IEPs, standardized test results, copies of report cards, health-related matters, and serious violations of school rules may be forwarded

What student records are kept after a student graduates?
Listen/look for: only information related to a student's name, address, graduation ranking, and courses completed

Why does the school keep such records?
Listen/look for: schools are required by law to keep student files for a period up to ninety-nine years

Who can see a student's records after he graduates?
Listen/look for: usually authorized school personnel that have authorization by the student (application for work) or legal warrant

What are the graduation requirements?
Listen/look for: every district has graduation requirements that the school board believes guarantee a quality education; many school boards will periodically review requirements and raise the bar if stronger emphasis is believed to be needed in some areas

PARENTS' RELATIONSHIP WITH THE SCHOOL

Parents and schools should adopt a unified team approach in an attempt to maximize the learning potential for every child. To be a valuable team player, parents must do their part to provide an enriching environment, be supportive of school goals, and cooperate as a willing partner in meeting the child's needs.

Teachers and principals cannot do the job alone. Before a child sets foot inside the schoolhouse door, his or her parents create a foundation that can aid or hamper a child's chance of success in school. The parents' behavior, values, and ethics become part of the child's makeup, affecting his or her actions in school. Many feel that student achievement is a reflection of and is greatly influenced by families and neighborhoods.

Just as parents are the child's first teachers, entrance into school does not sever that relationship. Continued support of the school ideals, academic standards, and position as a role model remain critical to school success.

Teachers rely on parents to support their actions and decisions. Communications sent home outline educational expectations and goals for the year. Parents' encouragement of appropriate behavior and study skills add credibility to the educator's position. Ridicule of rules, disregard for expectations, and displays of disrespect for the educational system not only add to a child's poor performance but also undermine the potential for success in school and hamper the development of skills needed for life. Certainly, parents play a crucial role.

Parents that are able to volunteer in schools have a unique opportunity to share in their child's education. They "share" the actual learning process with the educator and can relish the discovery of a wider world within their child. Parents unable to participate in their child's education at school can gain great insight by assisting with homework, rewarding good academic performance, and showing a keen interest in their child's school activities. To assist in school, parents need to do the following:

- Keep lines of communication open.
- Clarify rumors to avoid misunderstanding.
- Support teachers' goals, decisions, and activities.
- Take as active a part as possible in school.
- Trust the actions of school officials.
- Attend parent–teacher meetings.
- Learn about school expectations.
- Make every effort to understand before reacting.
- Avoid unconditional support for their child in the face of contradictory evidence.
- Wait to hear the school's version of events before overreacting.
- Assist the child without doing work for the child.
- Remember that teachers and principals are normally well intentioned.
- Be careful of rumors—they usually are based on someone's interpretation.
- Look into the facts before forming an opinion.
- Share information that could have an effect on your child's performance.
- Ask questions for clarity of understanding.
- Think before acting, listen before talking, and wait before rushing to judgment.

HOW TO CONTACT THE SCHOOL

From time to time, parents need to contact schools for any one of a variety of reasons. When this contact is necessary, it is important that parents follow basic guidelines to facilitate obtaining the information requested. When requesting information from schools, the following is important:

- Make certain what you want is available.
- Personalize the message.
- Clearly state the request.
- Clearly state why it is needed.
- Clearly state when it is needed.
- Thank the individual for his help.

When parents object to something or want to appeal a decision, parents should do the following:

- Get the facts first.
- Check the reasoning behind the issue.
- Consider the decision carefully.
- Put your concerns in writing (follow the previously listed guidelines).
- Thank the individual for considering your position.

When notifying the school for any reason, the following is important:

- Contact the correct person or office.
- State the facts related to the notification.
- State where you can be contacted to clarify.
- Thank the individual for her help.

VOLUNTEERING IN SCHOOLS

Many schools welcome parents and nonparents as volunteers. The type of volunteers needed ranges from providing special help for remedial students to assisting in the lunchroom and from working in the library to helping with classroom parties. Regardless of the duties assigned to volunteers, work in schools requires a degree of commitment, reliability, and attention to confidentiality issues. Parent volunteers must remember that they are in school to assist where needed. It is not the time or place to intrude upon the instruction of their child, receive special treatment from their child's teacher, or work only with their own child.

Once assigned as a volunteer, the parent needs to be accountable. Being reliable and consistent in coming to school on the scheduled day(s) and completing the work delegated is expected of all volunteers. A note of caution: Confidentiality rules mandate that what happens in school remains in school. Volunteers that find it necessary to discuss the behavior of students, performance of teachers, family concerns of students, or other school-related matters would no doubt be asked to leave.

Questions to Consider

Who can volunteer in the school?
Listen/look for: parents are invited to volunteer at most schools; well-meaning parents with a desire to help children can usually be of help in cafeterias, libraries, classrooms, and offices; volunteers are most often found at the elementary school level, but they are very useful in the secondary schools as well

What are the responsibilities of volunteers?
Listen/look for: it depends on where the volunteer is assigned; usually monitoring students, helping individual students, shelving books, and assisting with clerical duties are the most common responsibilities of volunteers

What about confidentiality issues?
Listen/look for: many schools require all volunteers to agree to abide by confidentiality regulations; often individuals working in schools hear and see things that must be kept private

Can volunteers discipline a child?
Listen/look for: usually no; parents understand when a teacher or principal disciplines their child; they often take exception to a vol-

unteer doing so; volunteers are usually told to bring the misbehavior to the attention of the teacher, and she will apply the behavior consequences

How can parents make certain that volunteers do not read about their private affairs?
Listen/look for: many things in schools are seen on a need-to-know basis; student files, medical records, custody papers, and other confidential records are available only to certified professionals that have a legitimate reason to view the record

What if a volunteer in the cafeteria yells at a child?
Listen/look for: volunteers are typically permitted to redirect a child that is acting out; however, yelling, screaming, and touching a student are off limits for volunteers

Can a parent ride the bus as a volunteer?
Listen/look for: often, insurance coverage permits only paid employees to ride school buses with the children

What clearances do parents need to be volunteers?
Listen/look for: the need for clearances is dictated by the amount of time a person is in contact with children; states regulate the need for clearances, and central educational offices usually can clarify the need for clearances

How does a parent obtain the clearances, and who pays for them?
Listen/look for: schools can supply information on applications for a clearance; usually it is up to the volunteer to pay any necessary fees

Do volunteers need a tuberculosis shot?
Listen/look for: the need for a tuberculosis immunization commonly depends on how often and in what capacity the volunteer is working; when volunteers handle food a tuberculosis immunization is often required

EDUCATIONAL JARGON

Every profession has it own jargon and terms. To those not involved in a particular profession on a daily basis, the jargon and acronyms used in the profession are often confusing. Education is no exception. The extensive use of educational terminology and jargon, while clear to principals and teachers, can leave parents scratching their heads. In some areas such as special education, the use of acronyms is common. When meeting with educators, parents should stop the educator and ask for definitions of unfamiliar terms to avoid misinformation and misunderstanding. Refer to the glossary near the end of this book for common definitions, keeping in mind that local definitions may differ in some cases.

Questions to Consider

What do all of the acronyms mean?
Listen/look for: check the glossary in this book; ask principals and teachers to define the words or acronyms they are using

Isn't special education confusing?
Listen/look for: special education regulations are often complicated and intricate to the onlooker; teachers and administrators engaged in teaching special education students and working with their parents are well informed of all federal regulations and state standards

SERVING ON SCHOOL COMMITTEES

Many schools have committees on which parents may serve. Safety committees, budgetary committees, school improvement committees, and other specific committees are only a few of the many committees in which some schools welcome parental involvement. Additionally, individual teachers may have activities planned in their classrooms where a parent helper is needed or a room mother is of value during special events. At the district level, committees are frequently instituted to obtain public input before school boards reach decisions. Boundary committees, report card committees, security committees, long-range planning committees, public relations committees, and financial review committees are only a few of the committees in some districts.

Questions to Consider

What committees does the school board have?
Listen/look for: school boards may have committees dealing with curriculum, personnel, finance, building and grounds, policy, or negotiations

What committees does the school have?
Listen/look for: many schools have committees dealing with safety, socials, the budget, or open houses

What if the committee recommends something the principal does not like?
Listen/look for: as stated previously, all committees serve an advisory function; while input from the committee is valuable, the principal makes the final decision after considering the alternative choices

Why does the principal have committees?
Listen/look for: principals create school committees to gather a wider range of ideas and suggestions as input into the formulation of educational decisions

Can a Parent Become a Member of a School Committee?

Schools and school districts interested in the active participation of parents will encourage them to become a part of school committees. Parents bring a unique perspective to committee work and provide an important viewpoint into a wide range of educational issues. Depending on the committee, the normal role of parents, as well as other members of the committee, is to discuss various approaches related to the needs of the district and then make a recommendation to the school board. The very nature of a committee to the board is advisory. Legally the school board must make the final decision regarding educational issues that affect the school programs. Likewise, the principal is the final decision maker at the school level. That does not mean that committee work is a waste of time. It is through such discussion, investigation of different approaches, and formation of recommendations that the educational leaders in a district reach valid decisions. Schools that mistakenly disregard committee recommendations are destined to lose parent support and have committee work viewed as a waste of time.

In some cases the committee may work without the active participation of the principal or the principal may set the guidelines and parameters for their work and then allow the committee to proceed. Regardless of the approach used, the principal and school district need the brainstorming of noneducators to reach final resolutions to problems and challenges.

Questions to Consider

Can a parent be on a committee?
Listen/look for: parents are invited to serve as committee members; parents interested in future membership on a committee should contact their principal

When do committees meet at school?
Listen/look for: normally committees meet during the school day when principal and teachers are available

Can a parent be on the ___(subject)___ committee?
Listen/look for: parents interested in a specific committee should express their wishes to the principal

Can parents help select teachers?
Listen/look for: the selection of new teachers can be a complicated process; after soliciting applications and screening and interviewing potential teachers, a recommendation is made to the superintendent and school board; most districts have found it beneficial if experienced educators are used for screening and interviewing candidates

Can parents help write the school rules?
Listen/look for: parents with suggestions related to school rules should share their ideas with the school principal; in some districts parents are involved in drafting rules; in most districts administrators, with advice from the school solicitor, formulate the school rules and regulations

Will the principal really listen to parents' ideas while on a committee?
Listen/look for: principals are interested in various viewpoints regarding rules, policies, and other areas; parents serving on committees must be reminded that they serve an advisory function only; legally and professionally, final decisions are made by the principal

CHAPTER 3

The Principal

THE IMAGE OF THE PRINCIPAL

Principals, like everyone else, have a life beyond school. They have families, attend social events, and follow the normal routine of most adults. Parents need to be reminded that the principal is entitled to a degree of privacy outside of the school.

The typical principal is present at school before school each day or after school or both. Scheduled appointments can often be conducted beyond the school day if it is more convenient for parents. However, principals appreciate advance notice and recognition that they may have other commitments after school. Keeping a principal into or after the dinner hour can be inconsiderate unless the meeting is such that it cannot be held at another time.

Questions to Consider

If parents want to talk to the principal during her lunch, can't they just come to the office?
Listen/look for: principals may be very busy during lunchtime; supervision of students in the cafeteria and meetings with teachers might already be planned; it is advisable to call the office and request a meeting during your lunchtime the following day

If parents cannot get to the school during the day, can they talk to the principal after school?
Listen/look for: principals are usually open to meeting with parents after school if meetings during school hours are not possible

Can parents have the principal's home phone number?
Listen/look for: some principals freely provide their home phone numbers; some have their phone numbers listed in local phone books; other principals, because of possible student harassment, reserve the right to have an unlisted phone number

Can parents talk to the principal about their child if they see him at a school football game?
Listen/look for: normally a football game or other extracurricular event is not the ideal place to discuss student progress in school; principals are often on duty at games and need to be attentive to activities at the event; while a quick question is permissible, it is recommended that you contact the school to set up an appointment to meet with the principal during the school day

Isn't the Principal Supposed to Be a Role Model for Students?

As stated earlier, principals, like all adults, have a life outside school. While educators are often held to a higher standard than other members of the community, it does not mean they must retire to their homes every night and be resigned to a life of solitude. Certainly a principal's behavior must conform to the values and morals of the community. The private life of a principal is of concern to the school board and community only to the extent that it affects his or her ability to administer a school. Unruly, illegal, or extreme behavior can become a subject of interest to the local school board, whose responsibility is to protect the image of the school district. Individual principals that continually behave in an unprofessional manner and that set a poor example could be viewed negatively and be subject to reprimand or other disciplinary measures.

Questions to Consider

How can a principal be a role model if he is seen in a bar?
Listen/look for: certainly teachers and principals are often held to a higher standard than members of the general public; parents need to be reminded that, as adults, principals are entitled to freedom of choice in their out-of-school activities as long as the activities are lawful and do not interfere with the educational environment of the school

What guidelines do principals follow in their private lives?
Listen/look for: most principals conduct themselves in a lawful and orderly fashion that reflects the morals and values of the community within which the school exists

Do principals have to conduct themselves properly in the community?
Listen/look for: yes, principals are expected to respect and display behavior that is conducive to that of a role model and educational leader; usually principals are held to a higher standard than others in the community

If a parent hears something negative about a principal, whom should she tell?
Listen/look for: parents should be careful repeating rumors; if a substantiated behavior is found to be objectionable to a parent, the principal's immediate supervisor or superintendent can be contacted

If a principal violates the law, can he lose his job?
Listen/look for: violation of the law may have an adverse effect on the principal's position; the severity depends on the type of violation committed by the principal; drug use, public drunkenness, lewdness, and other serious illegal actions can result in dismissal of a principal and, in severe cases, the loss of state certification

Are principals given drug tests?
Listen/look for: normally school principals are not required to take drug tests

Can a principal publicly support a political candidate?
Listen/look for: principals do not typically give up their rights as citizens when taking the position as an administrator; however, many

school principals choose not to openly support candidates running for school board

What Are the Qualifications to Be a Principal?

Various states have differing requirements for the position of public school principal. In most states, a principal must have been a teacher for a specific period of time. Special training must have been successfully completed in accredited colleges. In many cases, principals have a master's or doctorate in education (EdD) or perhaps a doctorate of philosophy (PhD). In most districts, they undergo a screening, an interview, and a review of credentials before being recommended to the school board for consideration. Often districts look for a person with experience in administration, but sometimes they hire from within the district if a highly qualified teacher applies. Beyond the required credentials, boards usually look for a candidate that has shown evidence of leadership; organization skills; the ability to meet established goals; the ability to communicate both orally and in written form; a rapport with students, parents, and staff members; and a willingness to devote the time and effort necessary to successfully lead a school staff.

Questions to Consider

What teaching experience must the principal have?

Listen/look for: in some states a minimum number of years as a teacher is required before an individual can become a principal; as teachers, potential principals must have had satisfactory ratings and advanced training

What college courses do principals complete?

Listen/look for: college courses for the principalship vary across colleges and universities; often principals take courses in school finance, supervision of personnel, evaluation of staff, school law, and other courses related to management of school personnel and development of curriculum; in many states a principal must serve an internship and pass a state test for her administrative certification

Does a principal have to live inside the school district?
Listen/look for: some school districts require a principal to live within the school district; some districts have no regulation relative to residency requirements; in all cases, the principal is expected to be available to respond to school emergencies and attend required school events

How long does it take to become a principal?
Listen/look for: as mentioned earlier, principals are required to teach for a number of years (perhaps five years); in addition they need to take courses related to administration (perhaps two years); in some districts a master's or doctorate is required (earning these degrees can take three to five years)

Does a principal have to be an educator?
Listen/look for: in most schools principals are educators; in some recent movements to reform schools, individuals with a business background have been employed as principals or building managers

What are the most important duties of a successful principal?
Listen/look for: providing a rich learning environment, obtaining adequate instructional materials for teachers, motivating students to learn, and being the instructional leader of the school are major duties; routinely, developing a class schedule, controlling student behavior, providing staff development, carrying out district policies, and protecting the school and its population are considered typical duties of successful principals

Why can't a good business-oriented individual run the school?
Listen/look for: in some school districts, individuals with a business background have been employed as principals; many feel that an effective principal needs experience in the classroom, actually teaching, to understand the educational process and be in a position to advise and assist teachers as they work with children

CHARACTERISTICS OF A GOOD PRINCIPAL

Principals need to be people persons. They need to be child oriented and interested in providing the best possible learning environment for the children. They must possess the ability to communicate impromptu and prepare and present researched documentation when requested. Good principals must maintain excellent time management skills, the ability to work under pressure, and the flexibility to adjust to continually changing circumstances.

Questions to Consider

Should a principal be a good people person?
Listen/look for: yes, a large part of a principal's job is dealing with parents, teachers, support staff, school board members, and members of the community

Are effective principals well liked by their staffs?
Listen/look for: many feel that excellent principals are respected, trusted, and seen as compassionate and supportive; most teachers respect a dedicated principal; becoming a principal to win a popularity contest is a flawed goal

Does a principal have to be a good public speaker?
Listen/look for: it is very helpful if the principal, as the educational leader of the school, is an organized, skillful public speaker

Is a good teacher automatically a good principal?
Listen/look for: not necessarily; many fine teachers do not have the ability to deal with the stresses and continual interruptions of the principalship; while good organization and a love of children are important in both positions, principals spend a great amount of time dealing with issues unrelated to teaching

Is a good principal automatically a good teacher?
Listen/look for: a good principal is usually a good teacher; in fact, many consider a principal a "teacher of teachers"; principals need to assist the teachers in the classroom, and being a good teacher is a great asset in meeting that goal

What Training Does a Principal Receive?

Most principals receive their basic training in teacher education classes. These undergraduate classes provide future principals with learning theories, methods used in teaching, and content knowledge. After teaching for a period of time, and if the desire to move into a leadership position exists, the potential principal must obtain additional training. Various graduate schools of educational administration require differing courses, but often graduate programs may require legal issues, school finance, supervision of personnel, principles of leadership, instructional leadership, and similar courses.

Normally, a principal must serve an internship similar to that required for teachers. This internship, completed under the guidance of a practicing school principal and in cooperation with an institution of higher learning, varies in length. Often as many as two hundred or four hundred hours of actual work in administrative areas is required. During the internship, potential principals are typically required to actively participate in the areas of finance, organization, staff relations, student issues, and other areas pertinent to the administration of a public school.

Questions to Consider

What undergraduate degree must a principal have?
Listen/look for: no specific undergraduate degree is required as a prerequisite for becoming a principal; excellent principals have undergraduate degrees in art, music, physical education, science, social studies, and other majors

What college did the principal attend?
Listen/look for: college or university backgrounds vary greatly

How long does a teacher have to teach before becoming a principal?
Listen/look for: the length of teaching time before becoming a principal varies across states

What degree(s) does the principal have?
Listen/look for: more and more school districts are requiring a master's degree and in some cases a doctorate as part of the application for a principal's position

What area did the principal specialize in?
Listen/look for: some administrators have advanced degrees in public school administration; some have master's of education; others earn an instructional leadership degree, doctorate of education, or doctorate of

philosophy; other degrees of a similar type may be represented by various principals

Can a parent review the principal's college transcript?
Listen/look for: college transcripts are confidential and not available to the general public

Aren't Principals Teachers?

Many people consider a principal a "teacher of teachers." This view may be valid if the principal demonstrates teaching approaches and instructs his or her staff members on educational issues. Monitoring classroom teaching performance, providing staff development, being involved in curriculum development, evaluating teaching skills, implementing new teaching techniques, and introducing new technology all represent strong teaching qualities on the part of the principal. In this respect, yes, principals are teachers.

Questions to Consider

Do principals work with and teach their staffs?
Listen/look for: yes, an important responsibility of a principal is working closely with the teaching and support staffs; mentoring, counseling, observing, and evaluating staff members are critical to effective school administration

Do principals teach classes in their schools?
Listen/look for: some principals occasionally teach classes in their schools; in most cases principals have daily duties that do not permit teaching students

Should the principal bring new ideas to the teachers?
Listen/look for: yes, staff development and curriculum improvement are continual needs to be met; some principals attend state and national conferences and bring new ideas back to their teachers; successful principals spent a great deal of time reading current reports of new programs, updating techniques, and investigating innovative strategies

Does the principal work with teachers to help them learn new programs?

Listen/look for: yes, mentoring teachers as they develop new programs is a responsibility of principals; many principals observe teachers as they pilot new programs and work as a team member in improving the instruction

How Visible Should the Principal Be?

Many educators feel that the visibility of the principal in the school building is critical to the operation of a successful school. Students and staff entering the building often feel a sense of calm and safety seeing the school principal in and around the facility. Additionally, the availability of the principal to see and talk to staff, meet and welcome children, and monitor the movement within the building can allow the principal to be a "problem preventer rather than a problem solver."

Questions to Consider

Should the principal be there to meet the children in the morning?

Listen/look for: most principals believe they should be visible to both students and staff as they enter the school building each day; knowing the principal is present provides a feeling of order and calm within a building

Should the principal be there at the end of the day to say good-bye to the students?

Listen/look for: just as it is important for a principal to be visible in the morning, it is equally important for his presence to be evident at dismissal

Is the principal in the hallways during class changes?

Listen/look for: administration by memo or spending the day in the office can lead to devastating results in many schools; the principal should be seen throughout the school and engaged in monitoring the learning process

Does the principal go into the classrooms during the day?
Listen/look for: while AWA (administration by walking around) helps monitor the overall climate in a school, the principal needs to be in the classrooms as much as possible; showing an interest in what the teachers are teaching and what the students are learning is imperative to the principalship

Does the principal go into the cafeteria at lunch to see the students?
Listen/look for: many principals make spot checks in the cafeteria during lunch; while it is difficult to spend the entire lunch period in the cafeteria, stopping by and chatting with the students in a less formal environment is beneficial

Is the principal at school board meetings?
Listen/look for: some districts require principals to attend district school board meetings; other districts do not require their attendance unless an issue related to their schools is on the agenda

DUTIES OF THE PRINCIPAL

There is little doubt that the principal's job can be a difficult one. Good use of time, honed organizational skills, and the ability to work effectively with staff members are great assets. But one of the most useful skills, and one of the most difficult to execute, is delegation of duties to others within the school. True delegation allows the principal to focus on the critical issues of the job. It permits others to develop their leadership skills and the opportunity to become part of the solution to challenges. The wise principal delegates responsibilities to his or her staff, drawing on their strengths and developing their skills in an effort to create a well-run school.

To many parents, the principal seems to live at the school. He or she is a disciplinarian, supervisor, counselor, and mentor, responsible for public relations, school climate, raising student test scores, and monitoring events before, during, and after school hours. It is impossible to be all things to all people, and it is equally impossible to have everything in the school done by one person.

Questions to Consider

Does the principal have to be at all school events?

Listen/look for: some school districts expect an administrator to be at all school events; elementary principals, usually without an assistant principal, often must attend all school-related events held at their buildings; at the secondary level, often with one or two assistant principals, the building principal can sometimes delegate supervision to one of his assistants; secondary schools customarily have many more evening events

Isn't the principalship stressful and frustrating?

Listen/look for: yes, at times the work of a principal can be stressful and frustrating; habitual behavioral problems, irate and unreasonable parents, and endless paperwork can create a negative workplace for a principal; every principal must find a way to deal with the duties and responsibilities of the position; for many principals, the self-satisfaction of serving a valuable purpose helps offset the little challenges that occur each day

How does a principal keep from "burning out"?

Listen/look for: stress and burnout are problems faced by many principals; in many cases, working with young people and the self-satisfaction of providing a wholesome environment for learning to take place, combined with hobbies or nonschool activities that balance school-related work, help principals sustain themselves; most principals love their work

Does the principal delegate tasks?

Listen/look for: yes, most principals delegate tasks to the lowest level possible; taking the time to train others to complete tasks is critical to finding enough time to get things done; of course, the principal is ultimately responsible for all work undertaken in the building

Does the principal have an assistant?

Listen/look for: school boards vary in their approval of hiring assistants at some levels; in many elementary schools, the building principal is the only administrator assigned to the facility; at some middle and junior high schools, one or two assistants may be hired to work with the building principal; at the high school level, most districts employ at least one or two assistants or deans of students

Does the central education office assist principals?
Listen/look for: yes, in most school districts the central office staff members are a great help to the building administrator; central office staff members (supervisors of curriculum, special education, personnel, testing, finance, and other specific areas) serve as valuable resources, advisors, and coordinators of activities among schools

Who Does the Principal Report To?

Normally a principal reports to either a director of education or assistant superintendent. As an example, an elementary principal might report to the director of elementary education in the district. Various districts have developed differing supervisory models and a variety of central office positions that supervise principals. Regardless of the person responsible for monitoring the performance of principals, building principals are held accountable for their behavior. Many districts mandate that principals work toward established district goals and meet other expectations as outlined in the principal's job description. Midyear and year-end evaluation sessions are often held to discuss a principal's success during the year regarding both the goals of the district and the successful operation of his or her building.

Questions to Consider

Who is the principal's supervisor?
Listen/look for: often there is a supervisor of principals or assistant superintendent that supervises principals; in some cases principals report directly to the superintendent; individual school districts organize their administrative supervisory model to fit their needs

Does the school board hire the principal?
Listen/look for: in most states the school board is either actually involved in the interviewing and selection of a principal or considers the recommendation of the superintendent; ultimately it is the school board that actually hires all employees in the district

How are principals evaluated?
Listen/look for: principals are evaluated in a variety of ways; some districts hold evaluation sessions in midyear and at the end of the aca-

demic year for principals; some districts are involved in merit plans whereby principals are evaluated on their performance; still others may engage in shadowing and on-site monitoring and evaluation of their administrative staffs

Do the teachers have input into the evaluation of principals?
Listen/look for: in some districts teachers are part of the evaluation system for principals; as the members of the educational team that work most closely with the principal, many feel teachers are the best judge of a principal's day-to-day performance

How Many Days Does a Principal Work Each Year?

The principal's work year varies greatly across school districts. From 187 days, following the teachers' work year schedule, to 360 days (hopefully with a few vacation days), the principal follows an established agreement with the school district. This includes the fact that most principals are responsible for their schools twenty-four hours a day, seven days a week. Often the number of contract days varies depending on the level of the building (elementary, middle, high school).

Questions to Consider

What is the length of the principal's work year?
Listen/look for: a principal's work year varies across districts; some districts require principals to work a full year (260 days with some vacation days built in); some have a 230-day work year (one month off in the summer); still others work 210 days (off approximately two months); regardless of the number of required workdays, most principals are expected to be available seven days per week, twenty-four hours per day

Do all principals in a district work the same number of days?
Listen/look for: this varies across districts; while many school districts require all administrators to work 260 days, more experienced administrators often have an increased number of vacation days; in other districts while secondary principals may work 260 or 230 days, elementary principals may work only 210 days

What is the length of the principal's workday?
Listen/look for: workdays vary from as little as eight hours on some days to well over twelve or fourteen hours on busy days

Does the principal have a vacation?
Listen/look for: school districts usually have agreements with administrators whereby they have some time off; most principals take the bulk of their vacation days during the summer

Does the principal go to conferences?
Listen/look for: in many school districts, principals may request permission to attend regional, state, or national conferences related to their work; new strategies or innovative programs, when approved by the school board, are often funded; as school funding is reduced, fewer requests for conferences are honored

Doesn't the Principal Work for Parents?

Actually, the school principal is an employee of the district school board. The school board sets salary, working conditions, and other parameters of the position. The voting members of the community, of course, elect the school board members. While principals are certainly accountable to the public, they are responsible to those that employ them: the school board.

Questions to Consider

Who does the principal work for?
Listen/look for: principals work for the school district under the authority of the school board; while it might appear that principals work for the parents, it is the school board and superintendent that are the direct employers

Isn't the principal a public servant?
Listen/look for: yes, because principals are paid through taxpayers' money they can be considered public servants

If parents object to something a principal did, can he be fired?
Listen/look for: the quality of the performance of a principal usually cannot be based on one incident (unless that incident is a serious

breach of school policy); individuals with grievances against a principal have every right to seek a resolution and refer the matter to those in a superior position; at the same time, principals are entitled to all rights of due process and a fair opportunity to defend themselves

Doesn't tax money pay the principal's salary?
Listen/look for: yes, a principal is paid a salary; in most cases, that is derived from local or state tax money

How can a principal do something parents disagree with if she works for them?
Listen/look for: principals, as stated previously, actually work for the school district and school board; principals make a multitude of decisions in the course of the school day, and some are unpopular with some members of the school community; in many cases every time a principal makes a decision, one of the parties disagrees with the solution

What if a parent has his attorney call the principal?
Listen/look for: in a majority of cases a principal is merely carrying out the policies of the district as approved by the school board; a call to a principal from an independent attorney will usually not affect the decision made by a principal; in some cases independent attorneys may contact the school solicitor to discuss school matters that will in turn be taken to the school board; the threat of a parent calling an attorney seldom alters the resolve of a principal

Does the Principal Ever Go Home?

It may seem to some parents that the principal is always at school. While many principals are at school a major part of the day, they do, of course, go home. It would not be far fetched to say that the school is the principal's "second" home. The long days and short nights experienced by principals are part of the job. Perhaps that is why, when a principal's position becomes vacant, the line of applicants is not exceptionally long.

Questions to Consider

How can a principal have a home life?

Listen/look for: successful principals achieve a balance between the busy job of the principalship and a rich and fulfilling family life; there is no doubt that principals need a life outside the school

What time does a principal arrive at school?

Listen/look for: most principals arrive early in the school day; often the time before the students arrive is a good time to meet with teachers and plan the activities of the day

How late does a principal work each day?

Listen/look for: principals often work until the dinner hour; some may go home for a period of time and then return for an evening school activity; few (if any) principals enjoy a 9 to 5 workday

Does the principal take work home?

Listen/look for: yes, principals often take work home as part of their effort to improve the school

Who Gives the Principal His or Her Authority?

The local school board, as either appointed or duly elected officials authorized to operate public schools, delegates the responsibility to the superintendent, who in turn delegates the daily operation of the school building to the principal. Additionally, the department of education in most states designates each school to be administered by a building principal.

Questions to Consider

What law gives the principal the authority to run the school?

Listen/look for: most state educational codes and laws specify the superintendent or his designee shall have authority to supervise schools; individual states may have various regulations related to the degree of a principal's authority

What law gives the principal the right to violate a child's rights?

Listen/look for: principals are not permitted to violate a child's civil rights; usually the discussion centers around what rights a child has or thinks he has; due process must be afforded to students, but no student has the right to interfere with another student's safety or right to learn

Can a superintendent overrule a principal's decision?
Listen/look for: yes, the decision of a superintendent can supersede a principal's decision; as the educational leader of the district, in most states, the superintendent has the final word in matters related to the education of children

Is the principal an officer of the state?
Listen/look for: no, a school principal is not an officer of the state; the local school board employs him

What Is the Principal's Highest Priority?

The priorities of a principal vary greatly across districts. A high priority is that of providing a safe learning environment in which students have the opportunity to reach their fullest potential. Within this overall goal, principals have a multitude of subgoals, from increasing the security of their schools to initiating a new math series and from improving student behavior to helping new teachers develop enhanced teaching skills.

Questions to Consider

What is the principal's highest priority for the year?
Listen/look for: every principal should have a set of priorities for her school; increased test scores, fewer students at risk, and reduced violence are better addressed when priorities are expressed as measurable goals

Does the principal have a long-range (five-year) plan?
Listen/look for: most school districts have long-range plans for improvement within the district; each principal should have expectations for their schools that coincide with the district plan

What is the principal's goal related to student test scores?
Listen/look for: principals are very aware of the test standings of their students; while the number of students receiving merit awards is noteworthy, many principals strive to improve the lower end of the testing range by increasing the scores of the lower achievers

How do the principal's priorities help the school reach its goals?
Listen/look for: many individual school goals are tied into the district goals; increased test scores, better communication, clearer understanding of special education regulations, more accountability of teachers, and reduced absenteeism are typical school/district goals

If the principal could change one thing about the school, what would it be?
Listen/look for: any realistic principal is aware of needed changes in the school; to be content with the status quo may display a lack of proactivity on the part of the administrator

Of what aspect of the school is the principal most proud?
Listen/look for: every principal is proud of his school; in most schools certain aspects are worthy of special attention and pride; principals are usually happy to share the pride they have in their students and staff members

Where does the principal see the school in ten years?
Listen/look for: proactive administrators with a vision project their goals to future years; even if the principal is not planning on being employed by the district ten years in the future, the principal should be setting goals and working toward a vision of improvement

Does the Principal Know How to Teach All of the Subjects?

No, the principal does not know the content of all subjects taught in his or her school. No one person can be fully knowledgeable of chemistry, social studies, math, industrial arts, home economics, and other areas taught in schools. However, the principal should know the qualities of a good lesson. Every lesson, no matter the subject area, should include those components accepted as critical to successful teaching. Introduction, student motivation, content knowledge, relevant homework, and summary of lessons taught are considered part of almost every class in almost every subject area.

Questions to Consider

How can a principal evaluate all teachers when he has not taught the subjects?
Listen/look for: certain characteristics are common to all good lessons; principals usually look for the elements that provide a quality education to children

What does the principal look for in a good lesson?
Listen/look for: principals often look for a quality educational experience that includes a creative introduction, motivation of students during the lesson, relevant content material, encouragement of student participation, use of innovative teaching techniques, a summary that pulls the lesson together, and a related assignment

Will the Principal Be Available to Talk to a Child?

Principals should welcome communication with children. Part of any principal's job is counseling children and working toward a smooth and successful academic year for each child. It is not uncommon for principals to spend large amounts of time with students that have misbehaved. But a wise principal will devote time each day to working with students at risk, special education students, and students not involved in misbehavior. Enhancing rapport with well-behaved students helps motivate students and serves as a stress reducer for the principal.

If a principal is too busy to meet and discuss positive issues with students, the principal may be inundated with problems and the negativity of school life.

Questions to Consider

If a child has a problem with a teacher, will the principal help and not prejudge?
Listen/look for: most principals believe their primary responsibility is to safeguard the safety and academic surroundings of the student; while principals care about and support their professional staffs, their main job is protecting students; principals should listen to concerns related to

teachers, investigate any accusations, and render decisions in the best interests of the student and school

Does a child have to set up an appointment to see the principal?
Listen/look for: normally a student with a concern can talk to the principal without an appointment; at times a principal may be involved in another activity that makes immediate conferring impossible

If a child talks to the principal, will the parents be called?
Listen/look for: in many cases, if the principal feels it will help the situation the parents will be called; as stated earlier, parents are important partners in a child's education; principals will usually keep a discussion confidential unless the information discussed could cause harm or danger to the student or another person

Will the principal believe a child if she tells him something?
Listen/look for: normally, unless the principal has a reason to disbelieve a child, concerns, accusations, and complaints are thoroughly investigated

Aren't Most Principals Men?

It is true that most secondary principals are male. At the elementary level, while many females hold the principal's position, males still dominate the administrative ranks. This most likely is a carryover from the days of the head teacher, historically male. Today, schools need both males and females in the principal's position. My experience has shown that while males can serve as tremendous role models for young men, women administrators can provide a source of comfort and degree of reassurance needed by girls. That is not to say that female principals cannot be successful at the secondary level. Many fine female principals administer at high schools across the nation.

Questions to Consider

Don't men make better principals?
Listen/look for: on the contrary, many excellent principals are female

Don't students respect a principal better if he is a "jock"?
Listen/look for: students will respect a fair, genuine principal that clearly states his expectations and then upholds reasonable consequences; whether a principal is a "jock" or not, respect is earned and not given because of athletic ability

How can a female principal maintain order?
Listen/look for: female principals have demonstrated a fine ability to maintain order; as long as the rules are clearly stated and the consequences fairly administered, a principal, male or female, will usually be successful

How can a female principal stop a fight between two students?
Listen/look for: seasoned principals use techniques that usually stop altercations without physically becoming involved; most principals and teachers recognize that stepping between two students engaged in fighting can result in serious personal injury

How many principals are men and how many are women in this district?
Listen/look for: every district usually has both female and male principals

CHAPTER 4

The Teacher

SELECTION OF TEACHERS

The qualifications to teach in the public schools normally consist of a four-year educational degree from an accredited institution of higher learning. Various courses are required, including methods courses on subjects taught, psychology, audiovisual and communications, specific subject major courses, and history of education. Additionally, student teaching experience is usually part of the requirements for receiving a teaching certificate.

Each school district looks for those characteristics that fit the needs of the district when interviewing candidates for teaching positions. The criteria for a specific teaching position may further screen candidates of equal qualifications until an applicant that meets the needs of the district, the requirements of the state department of education, and the plans of the building principal is selected.

Questions to Consider

Are all of the teachers in the school certified to teach their subjects?
Listen/look for: all teachers in a school should be properly certified; emergency certificates should be allowed only in subjects where fully certified teachers are in short supply

Are any of your teachers on an emergency certificate? Why?
Listen/look for: emergency certificates, usually issued by the secretary of education upon a superintendent's request, should only be found

when certificated teachers are not available; in those subjects (often the sciences) a certified teacher should be hired as soon as possible

From what colleges did the teachers in the school graduate?
Listen/look for: public schools located near colleges that offer education certification often have an overabundance of applications from that college; many feel it is better to have a variety of colleges represented on a faculty

How Are Teachers Selected?

Most principals feel the most critical element affecting the education of children is the employment of a quality teaching staff. Principals interested in obtaining the very best teachers make a great effort to recruit, screen, interview, and recommend highly qualified candidates for vacant teaching positions. The hiring of a teacher that proves to be ineffective in the classroom, unprepared in curricular areas, or unwilling to meet district expectations can educationally harm many children before the teacher is dismissed. To ensure that children receive the very best education, the very best teachers are essential.

Questions to Consider

What criteria does the district use to select teachers?
Listen/look for: some districts look for a high quality point average (QPA) from the college attended; some look for teaching experience in a particular subject or grade level; some districts are looking for a person with computer knowledge; letters of reference are checked; many search for a person with a sparkle in her eye that denotes an enthusiasm for teaching and a love of children

Is there a minimum quality point average for employment in the district?
Listen/look for: some districts require a 3.0 QPA; some districts limit hiring to teachers that have achieved at least a 3.5 QPA; regardless of the QPA required, college grades are only one of the indicators of an outstanding teacher

What is tenure?
Listen/look for: in some states teachers are awarded tenure once they have completed two or three years of satisfactory teaching; in some states tenure is valid for ninety-nine years; once tenure is confirmed the teacher is protected by special legal procedures

Are all of the school's teachers on tenure?
Listen/look for: in most districts where tenure is given, the majority of the teaching staff has achieved it; teachers found to be incompetent or lacking in the required skills to be a teacher should not reach a tenured status

Do teachers take state tests on competency?
Listen/look for: most states require a teachers' test before certification of a teacher takes place; more and more states are now requiring experienced teachers to take competency tests to maintain their teaching certificates

Do teachers have to take a drug test before they begin teaching?
Listen/look for: no, normally teachers do not have to take a drug test before they begin teaching; teachers normally must have a physical examination as part of being employed

Are teachers in the school well versed in their subject areas?
Listen/look for: based on the achievement tests administered, teachers have demonstrated competency in their subject areas; when teachers are observed and evaluated by the principal, they demonstrate a keen knowledge of their subject material

Is there an interview process?
Listen/look for: yes, but the interviewing process for hiring teachers varies from district to district; in some cases administrators interview potential teachers; in some districts teachers may be included on the interview team; and in some districts parents are also part of the team

Do teacher substitutes have an advantage in applying for a position?
Listen/look for: in many districts an individual that has substituted for a teacher has the advantage of having been observed by a principal in the district; firsthand knowledge of a candidate's abilities is useful and may supply information helpful in the selection of the successful candidate;

other than the firsthand knowledge that substituting may provide, school districts should always look for the best qualified candidate

Are potential teachers observed before being hired?
Listen/look for: most principals would welcome the opportunity to observe the effectiveness of a teacher applicant; in most cases it is impossible for the principal to observe a teacher in another district or an individual that has recently graduated from college

How Are Staff Members Screened to Work in the School?

School districts receive many more applications for employment than they could possibly honor. Thus, there must be some mechanism for screening or narrowing the number of applicants to those that best meet the needs of the district. This mechanism, different from district to district, usually includes the completion of an application and submission of the proper clearances and letters of recommendation. After these documents are submitted to the personnel office, a process is undertaken to further reduce the number of potential candidates. In some school districts, this is completed by teams of administrators reading and ranking the applicants in respect to qualifications, experience, quality point average (QPA), references, and other indicators relevant to the vacant position.

Once this part of the screening is completed, the most likely candidates are invited to interview for the position. The interview session usually consists of at least ten applicants for each position. The team of interviewers should then ask similar questions of all candidates and, based on the applicants' documentation and the information from the interview, choose a candidate for recommendation to the superintendent.

Questions to Consider

When do you interview and hire new staff?
Listen/look for: interviewing is often an ongoing process in some districts; knowing the candidates available in a district allows for better planning; usually a month or two before school opens becomes very busy, with increased numbers of applicants interviewed

Do you have to substitute teach in the district before getting a job?
Listen/look for: no; while many applicants for positions have substituted in the district previously, some have taught in other districts, and some are new teachers directly out of college

Why don't some of your substitute teachers ever get a contract?
Listen/look for: often substitute teachers become disheartened when they are passed over for a permanent position within the district; when openings occur, the district attempts to select the best candidate available; sometimes an individual that has substituted in the district is not the best candidate

Who screens the applications?
Listen/look for: screenings are completed in various ways; sometimes groups of administrators screen and narrow the field of applicants; personnel departments in some districts narrow the list of candidates; and in some districts computer-generated lists assist in screening potential candidates

What Personal Information Can Be Shared about a Child's Teacher?

The credentials and application forms of those applying for employment are confidential. The U.S. Constitution protects against the unwarranted invasion of a person's private matters. The applications of workers may only be read by those responsible for hiring. In the case of schools, this would pertain to principals, school board members, and other individuals involved in the hiring process.

Questions to Consider

How many years has ___(specific teacher)___ taught?
Listen/look for: this information is usually available to a parent

How many years has ___(specific teacher)___ taught this grade (or subject)?
Listen/look for: this information is usually available to a parent

What experience does a ___(specific teacher)___ have?
Listen/look for: experience is a wonderful thing if the teacher has grown and developed during those years of teaching; new teachers directly out of college also offer innovative teaching skills and an enthusiasm for their new positions

How many of the teachers have master's degrees?
Listen/look for: this information is usually available to a parent; caution must be given that the number of master's degrees on a staff does not necessarily indicate the quality of the instruction

What Does Certification Mean?

Certification is the term used by the state to indicate that an individual has met the requirements to engage in some type of specialized profession. In the case of education, it indicates that the holder of a certificate has met the state department of education's requirements for teaching, in a specific subject area or grade level, or has received a specific certificate such as reading specialist, behavioral specialist, or counselor. In addition, principals, superintendents, and many positions at central office require additional training and specialized certification.

Questions to Consider

Do all of your teachers have their permanent certification?
Listen/look for: most of the teachers have permanent certification as a result of having met the state requirements; those teachers that do not presently have permanent certification are currently engaged in courses to meet permanent certification requirements

What certification is needed to be a principal?
Listen/look for: most states require an individual to have some teaching experience and have completed specially designed graduate classes for successful management of schools and their instructional programs

What certification does the principal hold?
Listen/look for: principals must be certified in some aspect of school administration; some may have a master's in school administration or

a similar area; some may have a PhD or EdD in some areas related to school administration

Can a teacher be moved from one grade level to another grade level?
Listen/look for: in some elementary schools the principal has the authority to move a teacher from one grade to another; in most secondary schools the principal is limited in the ability to move teachers because of certification issues; teachers can often be moved within departments at the secondary level if they are properly certified to teach in the reassigned area

How can a certification be withdrawn?
Listen/look for: in most states, the secretary of education can take steps to remove the certification of a teacher found guilty of a violation covered under the state educational code

Who Interviews Teachers?

After the screening process is completed and a number of candidates are selected to be interviewed, appointments are scheduled to meet each potential teacher.

The interview team varies from district to district. In some, a team of administrators talks with the candidates; in others, teachers may serve on the team; and in some others, parents may be part of the interviewing process. Regardless of the team's composition, a number of individuals are involved to provide a wider platform on which to base a recommendation.

Questions to Consider

Do parents ever participate in interviewing potential teachers?
Listen/look for: yes, sometimes they do participate; however, many districts do not involve parents because of the time involved, confidentiality issues, and the specificity of the questions

What if a good candidate for a position cannot be found?
Listen/look for: in the event that a fully certified, qualified teacher cannot be found to fill an open position, an emergency certificate can often

be obtained; teachers working under an emergency certificate are expected to meet the curriculum standards of the board

Are teachers required to teach a class before being hired?

Listen/look for: in many cases, teachers, other than those substituting in the district, are not observed teaching; because candidates are often interviewed in the summer, observation of teaching is not possible

How does a principal know a teacher is good without seeing him teach?

Listen/look for: administrators experienced in the interviewing process develop a sense of the qualities needed to be a successful teacher; references from principals that have seen the candidate teach are helpful; in most cases new teachers are hired on a probationary status until they are observed and evaluated by the principal

Do teacher candidates take a district test before being hired?

Listen/look for: in some districts teachers are required to complete a test either when applying or before interviewing

Is nepotism a problem in this district?

Listen/look for: nepotism has been seen as a problem in some districts; in some districts there are policies against nepotism; in other districts it apparently is not a concern

Who Hires Teachers?

The actual hiring of a teacher is the responsibility of either the superintendent or the district board of school directors. The superintendent often recommends candidates to the board for their consideration, and upon a recorded vote of the members present, and if a majority of the members vote in the affirmative, the successful candidate is hired for the advertised position.

Questions to Consider

Can a parent find out the vote of individual board members related to the hiring of a specific teacher?

Listen/look for: all votes cast by school board members are part of the public record

How does the board know the superintendent's recommendation is a good one?

Listen/look for: school board members either trust the judgment of their superintendent or they do not; some boards will question the recommendation of a particular candidate; some boards will vote not to hire the recommended candidate and request that additional interviewing take place

If a teacher had a problem in another district, can she still work in this district?

Listen/look for: teachers that experience difficulties in one district may find it difficult to find employment in another district; school districts often contact a teacher's previous principal for work history and past performance

What if the board does not want to hire a specific candidate?

Listen/look for: boards always have the right to reject a recommendation

Can a successful candidate decline the employment?

Listen/look for: yes, even after the board has approved a candidate's selection the candidate can decline the employment

Can one board member veto a recommendation?

Listen/look for: usually a majority of the board is required for successful employment; a single board member, having only one vote, cannot solely veto a candidate

How much influence does the board have on who is recommended?

Listen/look for: members of the school board should not attempt to influence the selection of a particular candidate; if a school district is interested in hiring the best candidate, pressure from a board member is unethical

Can Parents Select a Specific Teacher for Their Child?

The selection of a teacher for a specific class is, in most cases, the decision of the building principal. For the principal to effectively operate his or her building, he or she must have the latitude to place teachers and students in appropriate classes. While many parents, especially at the elementary level, might like to choose their child's teachers, the need to have the size of classes balanced makes it very difficult. Also, parents wanting a certain teacher may not be the best people to select the teacher–student mix. Often the common reasons for requesting a certain teacher are past unpleasant experiences with another teacher or the knowledge that a certain teacher is an outstanding educator.

Many principals will listen to parent concerns if they have had a negative relationship with a teacher in the past. However, the final decision of any placement lies with the principal, as the instructional leader in the school. All parents would like their child placed with the best teacher in the school, but consider the ramifications of such a request. That "best" teacher (as perceived by parents) would end up with classes of fifty or sixty. This is totally unacceptable. It has been my experience that most, if not all, teachers in a building are good, substantial teachers; none would purposely hurt or interfere with a child's learning. It is the principal's job to see that all of his teaching staff are qualified and performing in an acceptable manner.

Questions to Consider

Can parents change their child's teacher if they don't like him?
Listen/look for: most public schools do not operate on a "pick your teacher" system; principals usually feel that all of their faculty are qualified and will do a good job; principals are trained to select qualified staff members and expect all teachers to meet the needs of all children

Can a child be assigned to a classroom with her friend?
Listen/look for: once again, schools usually do not operate on a pick your teacher system

If a parent has had a problem with a teacher in the past, will his child be assigned to her?
Listen/look for: few principals want to begin a school year with a child assigned to a teacher that has had a previous confrontation with the child's parent; while it is usually not possible to pick a child's teacher, it may be possible to avoid having a child assigned to a particular teacher if there is a valid reason

If a child needs a male teacher, can he be assigned to one?
Listen/look for: principals are reasonable people; if they talk with the parent and agree that a male figure would be helpful in a child's educational life, assignment to a male teacher may be possible within certification limits

If a child relates better to women, can he have a female teacher?
Listen/look for: as stated previously, most principals are reasonable, but they also realize that children need exposure to a variety of personalities; depending on the circumstances, a special assignment may be possible within certification limits

SUPERVISION OF TEACHERS

Like all employees, teachers must be supervised. Principals are typically the individuals professionally, legally, and ethically responsible for monitoring teachers and, when necessary, authorized to take steps to correct or remove ineffective personnel. The process used in the supervision of teachers varies across districts, but most school boards expect building administrators to be fully aware of the activities taking place in all classrooms. To watch over a large staff can be a difficult task. Many principals monitor their buildings by walking around during the school day, making spot checks in classrooms, formally observing the teaching process of all teachers, and reviewing the test results of students.

No supervisory model is perfect. In an effort to maintain the quality of education, as stated earlier, a thorough screening and interviewing process helps select the best teachers possible. It is the principal's duty, after teachers are hired and in their positions, to continually make certain that children are provided with an excellent education taught by qualified, caring teachers.

Principals normally are the primary supervisors of teachers. As the instructional leaders in their schools, it is the principals' responsibility to know the curriculum, be well versed in teaching strategies, and closely monitor the performance of all staff members. Typically, principals observe teachers as they teach and make recommendations regarding the improvement of instruction.

The assessment of teaching practices is a primary concern to principals. Additionally, accuracy of reports, adherence to school rules, and relationships with students and parents are important to a successful school and are often part of expectations for teachers.

Questions to Consider

How often do principals observe teachers?

Listen/look for: in many school districts principals are required to make formal observations of each experienced teacher at least two times per year; some beginning teachers are observed four or more times until they have adjusted to the school and achieved permanent status; if a teacher is having a problem, the principal may observe his classes several additional times each year

Are evaluations completed in a fair and unbiased manner?

Listen/look for: effective and professional principals attempt to evaluate all staff in an unbiased and fair manner; the impartial judgment and recognized expertise of the principal are crucial if the school is to have a harmonious working environment

Does a teacher's evaluation affect her salary?

Listen/look for: normally a teacher's salary is not affected as a result of an evaluation; exceptions may occur if the teacher is working under a merit plan, is involved in a career ladder system related to salary increases, is not rehired as a department head, or is under a supplemental contract such as coaching

Can a teacher really be dismissed?

Listen/look for: yes, incompetent teachers can be dismissed; normally a period of remediation and assistance is offered and time for improvement allowed; if the teacher continues to fail to meet district expectations, he can be referred to the board for dismissal proceedings; of course, extreme behavior on the part of the teacher could result in immediate suspension leading to dismissal

What constitutes a reason to revoke a teacher's certificate?

Listen/look for: in some states teachers may have their teaching certificates revoked (after due process rights are followed) for incompetency, cruelty, negligence, immorality, or intemperance

How does a principal know what is happening in the classroom when she is not there?
Listen/look for: principals gain a sense of what is happening in classrooms by walking around the building, stepping into classrooms periodically, monitoring lesson plans, talking with students and parents, and making formal observations

What happens if a teacher is not following the curriculum?
Listen/look for: principals routinely monitor lesson plans to make certain the curriculum is being followed; periodic observations of test results as well as classroom observations help gauge the degree of adherence to the curriculum

How many teachers does a principal supervise?
Listen/look for: the number of teachers under the supervision of a principal varies greatly; in some schools, particularly at the elementary level, the principal may be the only administrator in the building and thus must supervise and observe all of the teachers; at the secondary level, assistants may help supervise and monitor teachers' performance; a ratio of thirty or more to one is not uncommon

What other staff members does a principal supervise?
Listen/look for: ordinarily principals are responsible for the supervision of all employees in his building; custodians, secretaries, educational assistants, and food service workers may report directly to the principal

Does a principal supervise teachers outside of the classroom?
Listen/look for: yes, the behavior and actions of teachers outside of the classroom are a concern for principals as well; rapport with parents, willingness to carry out assigned duties, concern for students throughout the school, and ability to complete reports on time are scrutinized by principals

Can a principal discipline a teacher?
Listen/look for: disciplining a professional teacher often requires extensive consultation and discussion before being implemented; teachers that are consistently late for work, display a lack of concern for following school rules, and habitually fail to complete assigned tasks may be warned, have letters placed in their files, be referred to the personnel department or superintendent, or in severe cases, be referred to the

school board for disciplinary action; in addition, the annual written evaluation of a teacher reflects her quality of performance during the school year

Can a parent report a teacher that is not doing his job?
Listen/look for: certainly, parents can and should report concerns related to teachers; parents should remember that occasionally what they hear from their child may be a child's perception rather than reality

Who Evaluates Teachers?

The test of effectiveness in the classroom can be a complex issue. First of all the abilities of the teacher must be measured. This can be addressed through on-site observations. The content of the lesson is directly related to the effectiveness of the lesson and must be in line with the board-approved curriculum. In many schools the effectiveness of classroom instruction is measured by monitoring the test results of students in various curricular areas.

The primary supervisor of the teaching staff is normally the school principal (as a delegate of the superintendent). He or she is responsible for all aspects of the instructional programs within the school. In addition, principals from other school buildings within the district may sometimes observe a teacher. Members of the central office administrative team or the superintendent may also observe teachers. Many times when a teacher is having a serious problem in the classroom, the school principal will request additional observations from other administrative staff members to remove any suggestion of bias.

Principals should meet with each teacher after the classroom observation to discuss the lesson presented. This is the time when recommendations are made and improved instructional techniques are discussed. At the end of the year some type of summative evaluation is normally presented to each staff member. This document can serve as reinforcement for excellent teaching, as a summary of the principal's assessment of needed improvements, or as needed documentation for possible dismissal.

Questions to Consider

Is the principal the only one that can evaluate teachers?
Listen/look for: superintendents are empowered by law to evaluate teachers, but in most cases they delegate that responsibility to principals, and as a result, principals are the primary evaluators of teachers; sometimes department heads, central office supervisors, and perhaps the superintendent may observe and evaluate teachers

Does the principal tell the teachers he is coming to observe them?
Listen/look for: some school districts prefer to give advance notice of pending classroom observations, while other districts feel teachers should be prepared to be observed at any time; many principals feel it is more professional to let teachers know when they are scheduled to be observed; it is very difficult for a poor teacher to present a quality lesson, with or without notice

How does the principal find time to observe and evaluate all of the teachers?
Listen/look for: time management is one of the most difficult areas for many principals to control; conscientious principals must carefully schedule their time to permit them to conduct the very important task of monitoring teacher performance

Can principals rank teachers?
Listen/look for: schools usually do not rank teachers; each teacher is considered a certified professional with the best interests of the children at heart; teachers are normally evaluated but not ranked

Where is the line between a poor and a satisfactory teacher?
Listen/look for: the ultimate test of satisfactory teaching lies in the answer to the question "Are the children learning?"; if children are learning but there are areas that the teacher can improve on, the principal can work to enhance them; if the children are not learning because of the teacher, immediate steps should be taken to mitigate the situation

What steps does the principal take to improve the effectiveness of teaching?
Listen/look for: often peer mentoring, the principal's suggestions, additional training, and repeated observations are helpful

Are Students Ever Asked How the Teacher Is Doing?

The use of student surveys in schools to measure teacher effectiveness is subject to question. The age of the students and the knowledge level of the students play a role in the validity of the results. In addition, care must be taken that a highly qualified teacher that sets high standards is not judged ineffective because of his or her strict standards. Furthermore, in some cases, a teacher that grades easily and operates a loose class may be highly liked by students, receive high marks on a survey, and yet be ineffective in delivery of the curriculum.

In some schools, in addition to classroom observations, student test results, peer review, and portfolios, high school students are requested to provide input into the overall evaluation of teachers.

Questions to Consider

Do principals ever ask the students how good a teacher is?
Listen/look for: surveying students regarding the quality of a teacher's performance is risky; at the elementary level, many feel the students are not knowledgeable enough to provide valid assessment; at the secondary level, some teachers fear that students will be unfair in their judgment and seek retaliation for poor grades or high expectations

Aren't students the best judge of how good a teacher is?
Listen/look for: possibly; often students have their individual perceptions related to a teacher's performance; because of possible flawed assessments, care must be taken when judging the validity of students' remarks

What If a Child Is Afraid of the Teacher?

Fear of a teacher is often based on inaccurate rumors and remarks from students previously taught by the teacher. In many cases the fear is unfounded and leads to unnecessary apprehension and dread for a new student. Parents of a student experiencing fear of a teacher should arrange a meeting with the teacher in question and discuss their child's perceptions.

Some students react negatively when called on too often. Many of us have memories of the dread we may have felt when we were called on to answer a teacher's question. Other students may express dissatisfaction when a teacher fails to call on them often enough. Basically, fear of a teacher, unless based on actual negative events, can usually be reduced through a parent–teacher discussion and strategies to overcome the student anxiety.

In cases where specific, justified reasons are expressed for the existence of fear, administrative intervention may be needed. Most would agree that a student that is fearful of a teacher performs poorly.

Questions to Consider

What if a teacher is mean?

Listen/look for: it depends on the definition of "mean"; a truly mean teacher does not belong in the classroom; a teacher that assigns challenging work, sets high expectations, and requires students to act responsibly is a treasure, not mean

What if a teacher calls on everybody but a particular child?

Listen/look for: calling on children for answers should generally be random and involve every student; parents that feel their child is not being called on should consult the teacher

What if a teacher moves a child to the front of the room without a good reason?

Listen/look for: in most cases there is a valid reason for the movement of a child to the front of the classroom; while the student may disagree with the move, most teachers feel the child needs more attention, more time on task, or more supervision

What if a child thinks the teacher does not like her?

Listen/look for: children that have a fear of the teacher or who feel disliked usually do not do well in school; parents should meet with the teacher and discuss the issue with the hope of rectifying the situation

What if a child says his teacher never commends him for his good work?

Listen/look for: recognition of student effort is encouraged in all schools; parents that feel their child's effort is not being recognized should sit down with the teacher and discuss techniques to acknowledge student effort

Can a parent arrange to sit in on her child's class?
Listen/look for: some teachers' contracts do not permit uncertified observers in the classroom; in most cases, a teacher will permit a parent to visit a class; multiple visits or regularly scheduled visits can be disruptive to the instruction in the classroom; in all cases the reasons for the visit must be clearly outlined and understood by all parties

What If the Teacher Is Rude to Parents?

There is no reason for any professional educator to be rude to a parent. While conversations with teachers may not always conclude as the parent would desire, professional ethics demand that teachers conduct themselves in an appropriate manner. However, parents that meet with educators with the intent of addressing them in a rude, threatening, or disrespectful manner should have no misapprehensions that teachers will sit back and take it. Most teachers are instructed to end any meeting that begins or escalates into a nonproductive, antagonistic encounter. Such meetings should be rescheduled with an administrator present.

Often children feel they are being treated unfairly. Typically, teachers have legitimate reasons for grades, test scores, or treatment of students. Concerned parents should bring the matter to the attention of the teacher and listen to the explanation.

In cases where the parent feels that the child has actually been treated unfairly, after meeting with the teacher, a meeting with the principal should be arranged.

Questions to Consider

What can be done if the teacher is rude and defensive to a parent on the phone?
Listen/look for: there is no reason for a teacher to be rude to a parent at any time; teachers are requested to cooperate with parents for the good of the child; teachers do become defensive if they feel they are being attacked; parents must remember that the best approach to talking with a teacher is a display of respect for a professional that is trying to help their child; cases of unprovoked rudeness should be discussed with the principal

What can be done if a teacher is abrupt and uncooperative?
Listen/look for: parents and teachers should be partners in the education of children; while teachers are to cooperate with parents to the extent possible, cooperation is a two-way street

What if a teacher continually blames a child's behavior on his home life?
Listen/look for: blaming a parent or a child's home life does not solve the problem; public schools must take and attempt to educate all children regardless of their home lives

What If a Teacher Does Not Communicate with Parents?

Open communication with parents should be a goal for all teachers. As stated earlier, education is a team effort that requires the cooperation of both the teacher and the parents. When communication is disrupted or does not exist between the two sides of this team, the child's education suffers.

After first speaking with the teacher, parents that continually find a lack of communication should consult the principal. It is recommended that the parents, in the interest of their child, make the extra effort to communicate with the educator. In some instances, the teacher may be busy with troublesome students and may innocently overlook routine messages from the parents of nonproblematic students.

Questions to Consider

What if a parent has tried to communicate with a child's teacher to no avail?
Listen/look for: if repeated attempts to communicate with a teacher go unanswered, a meeting with the principal and teacher is justified

Why did a teacher not notify parents that their child was failing?
Listen/look for: in many schools a midterm report is sent home alerting parents of the potential grades of students at the end of the grading period; any failing grade or any drop in grades (an A to a C) should be communicated to parents in an effort to help the child improve

If parents take the time to call teachers, why can't teachers call them back in the evening?

Listen/look for: teachers are expected to return calls to parents, but teachers may not receive the request to call a parent in a timely fashion; a teacher may not have a planning period that day, or attempts to reach a parent may not be fruitful; many teachers do call parents in the evening; in most cases there is no requirement that teachers call parents from their home; parents should call and leave a message a second time

What If a Teacher Refuses to Meet with the Parents?

Teachers are busy people. But meeting with parents, at appropriate times, is part of the teacher's responsibility in most schools. When adequate notice is given it is reasonable to expect teacher cooperation. Parents should keep in mind that while communication with parents is desired and teachers normally have a professional responsibility to comply, meetings outside of the teacher's workday are not mandatory.

Questions to Consider

Can a parent meet with a child's teacher before school, during the teacher's lunch, or after school?

Listen/look for: meeting with a teacher before the school day begins is often possible; teachers are usually open to adjusting their schedules if they have adequate time to do so; in most states, teachers are permitted at least a thirty-minute duty-free lunch; many teachers will meet over lunch or meet briefly after a quick lunch if advance notice is given; staying after school can cause problems for a teacher with small children at home; usually a teacher will plan to stay for a short time to meet parents if there is no other time possible

If a parent has had a confrontation with a teacher in the past, does the teacher still have to meet with the parent?

Listen/look for: if a teacher has had a major confrontation with a parent in the past, it is usually wise, for both parties, to have the principal sit in on subsequent conferences

Is time set aside for parents to meet with teachers?
Listen/look for: most schools have open houses, parent orientations, and parent coffee klatches for parents to meet and briefly chat with teachers; discussion of a specific nature should be scheduled for another time

Does the principal always sit in on parent–teacher conferences?
Listen/look for: no, principals with large teaching faculties cannot possibly sit in on all parent–teacher conferences; normally principals are happy to attend if either the teacher or the parent requests their presence

Can a parent bring a boyfriend or girlfriend to a conference?
Listen/look for: as a parent you may bring anyone you choose to a conference; however, the responsibility of the principal is to discuss matters with the custodial parent or adoptive parent; comments by others may or may not be considered germane to the discussion; parents need to know that confidentiality is lost when multiple individuals are part of the discussions

How do parents schedule an appointment with the superintendent?
Listen/look for: call the district administration office and request a meeting with the superintendent; either the secretary will set up the meeting or the superintendent will call to confirm; it is always helpful if the reason for the meeting is shared so that the superintendent can obtain background information often needed in the discussions

Is It a Good Idea for a Parent to Meet with a Child's Teacher?

Teachers, like principals, are eager to meet with parents. They realize that the parent is a vital part of the team in educating a child. Teachers will normally arrange to meet parents before or after the school day or during their preparation period. While time is limited, parents can usually schedule a meeting within a day or two of their request. When time is not available to meet in person, many teachers will phone parents to discuss issues. This may save the parents a trip to the school and still answer their questions.

Questions to Consider

Can parents have a meeting with all of their child's teachers?
Listen/look for: in almost every school, meetings between teachers and parents are routine

What If the Teacher Lacks Understanding of the IEP?

An individual education plan (IEP) is a legal agreement between the school and the parent. As such, school officials are legally required to carry out the goals of the IEP.

Teachers and principals involved in providing the strategies and adaptations outlined in the IEP must know the contents of the plan and the role they play.

When a parent feels that a teacher is not following the agreed upon plan, an immediate meeting should be scheduled with the special education teacher. The special education teacher is the case manager of the IEP and, along with the principal, is responsible for its implementation. If discussions with the teacher do not resolve the issue, the building principal should be contacted to intervene. Ultimately, it is the principal that is charged with the proper execution of the IEP.

Questions to Consider

What teachers are allowed to read a child's IEP?
Listen/look for: IEPs are confidential contracts between the parent and the school; as such, only staff members with a need to know are entitled to read a child's IEP

What if a teacher does not meet the goals of the IEP?
Listen/look for: in many schools the special education teacher and principal are the liaison between the regular teachers and the parent; concerns related to the meeting of goals in an IEP should be discussed with the special education teacher; if goals are not being met, it is possible to have a meeting with the principal and teachers and, if needed, open up the IEP to adjust goals

Can parents meet with the teacher and review the IEP?
Listen/look for: IEPs may be reviewed and updated at the request of the parent; contact the special education teacher or principal of the school; whenever an IEP is rewritten, it is an IEP meeting; a local education agency (LEA) must be present at all IEP meetings

Will all of a child's teachers modify their curriculum if needed?
Listen/look for: once agreed to and signed by the LEA the IEP must be carried out as written; if adaptations to the regular curriculum, modifications to existing programs, extended test taking time, or special arrangements are outlined in the IEP they are legally mandated

Can the special education teacher explain the IEP to the other teachers?
Listen/look for: yes, the special education teacher is the advocate for the special needs child and the liaison between the school and the parent

What is the least restrictive educational environment?
Listen/look for: the least restrictive educational environment means that the special needs child is to be placed in regular classes to the extent possible

What Is Standardized Testing?

Today, many schools are judged on the scores students achieve on standardized tests. Some educators feel that this basis for judgment is unfair because the public schools must take every student that lives within their attendance area. Further, they have no control over the background and desire to learn of their students. Educators point out that many private schools can be more selective in students attending, and in most cases, students dismissed from private schools return to the public school system. Regardless of the viewpoint, schools are being judged based on their students' test scores.

With the enactment of No Child Left Behind (NCLB), all states have established testing instruments to measure their student population against established minimum levels. But many question the ability of any school to leave no child behind, considering the fact that some children cannot, regardless of valiant efforts, meet criteria demanded in the law. Some even point out that it may be statistically impossible to meet some states' requirements. Federal funding, state money, and in some cases, management of the school district may depend on meeting the goals of NCLB.

Questions to Consider

What is testing all about?
Listen/look for: standardized testing is used to compare the abilities of groups of children in many schools across the nation; comparisons are often in terms of national norms, state norms, and local results; parents can gauge the test results of their child in relation to other children of the same age in the nation

What is No Child Left Behind?
Listen/look for: No Child Left Behind (NCLB) is a federal law, signed by President Bush in 2001, that was designed as a major step toward improving student achievement in school; although a controversial law, NCLB mandates higher educational standards, annual testing of children, analysis of test data, and the dispensing of rewards or punishments for schools depending on their degree of success; questions have arisen regarding the practicability of the testing used in some states

What areas are important to test?
Listen/look for: most feel it is important to test for mastery of skills; creative problem solving as well as logical thinking, as opposed to reciting facts and statistics, are often tested; additionally communication skills, interpretation of information, and making sound judgments are considered important by many

Does the principal monitor the standardized test scores of students?
Listen/look for: effective principals help students prepare for standardized testing and monitor the results; many school districts require principals to measure the achievement of their students against previous students and longitudinally (looking at individual students over several years)

How has the school ranked in recent PSSA and NCLB (or other) tests?
Listen/look for: most states maintain records of a school's past standardized test results for reference; parents can normally obtain the result of a recent testing period and then compare it with past years; often school boards will publish the results of state tests in the local media

Can teachers teach anything they want in their classes?
Listen/look for: teachers certainly have academic freedom to teach a lesson in a manner that is appropriate to the content and that encompasses their own style of teaching; the content taught in the classroom is controlled by the approved curriculum, the demands of the district, and the monitoring of the administration

What steps are taken to help a poor teacher improve?
Listen/look for: often additional observations and recommendations are made to the teacher; peers may assess the need for improvement; central office staff may be invited to observe and suggest improvements; principals from other buildings may observe; in-depth discussions will undoubtedly be conducted to assist the teacher in meeting the expectations of the school district

If teachers have tenure, what good is the principal's evaluation?
Listen/look for: the mere fact that a fellow professional is evaluating their performance and the desire to do the best job possible is a motivator for some teachers; most teachers are hungry for new methods and ideas and value the principal's input related to improvement of instruction

What about a Teacher's Behavior in the Classroom?

Certainly, a principal cannot be physically present in all classrooms at all times. Teachers must be trusted to use professional judgment, appropriate techniques, and common sense. In ninety-nine out of one hundred cases this is exactly what occurs. In cases where the administration discovers that a teacher varies from accepted and approved procedures, action must be taken. In some cases teachers can be worked with to improve (e.g., they can be assisted by a peer); in severe cases, teachers can be suspended or dismissed following legal procedures.

Questions to Consider

If a parent reports that a teacher is experiencing a problem, will the principal take action?
Listen/look for: yes, principals want to help teachers experiencing a problem as soon as possible; keep in mind that a problem from a student's eyes may not be a problem from the school's perspective

What happens if a teacher swears in class?
Listen/look for: if the accusations are found to be true the teacher is normally warned that the behavior is unacceptable; continued behavior of this nature can result in disciplinary action

If a parent hears that his child's teacher is talking negatively about his child to other teachers, what can be done?
Listen/look for: be careful of believing rumors; if substantiated facts indicate that a teacher is acting in a negative manner, a conference with the teacher and the principal is called for

What happens if a teacher inappropriately touches a student?
Listen/look for: if the accusations are found to be factual, the teacher is usually dismissed and police charges filed; the process can be a long and difficult one if the teacher denies the allegations; school districts and communities must be careful not to prejudge the teacher because false claims have been made by students in the past; a prudent principal follows up on every accusation of this nature; both teachers and children must feel that they are safe from false accusations in school

What if a teacher continually talks about personal matters in class?
Listen/look for: discussing relevant issues from a teacher's life may be appropriate in some classes; excessive conversations of a personal nature may need to be curtailed if they become the focus of the lesson

What if a teacher says derogatory things about a student's name in class?
Listen/look for: students are expected to show respect for their teachers; all teachers are expected to display equal respect for their students; nicknames, alterations of family names, and private pet names for students have no place in a classroom

What if a teacher shows a movie with objectionable language in it?
Listen/look for: teachers should preview all videos and movies before showing them in class; generally, only PG movies should be shown at the elementary level; videos and films relevant to the lesson should be part of the approved curriculum

What if a teacher backs a child into a corner and leaves him no choice but to strike out?
Listen/look for: under no circumstances should a student strike a teacher; students that find themselves being pushed into a corner (unacceptable behavior on the part of the educator) should follow the adult's directives and report the incident to a school official later; teachers are not permitted to harass, badger, or otherwise place students in a position where they feel they must fight back; parents that feel this type of behavior is taking place in school should notify the principal

If a child's teacher is continually assigned student teachers (uncertified), how can students be taught adequately?
Listen/look for: most colleges and universities have guidelines regarding how student teachers are to be used in the classroom; student teaching is a learning experience and as such teachers in training should only be assigned to master teachers; a student teacher normally is kept under the watchful eye of an experienced teacher, not turned loose to learn on her own

What if a teacher shows television programs all the time?
Listen/look for: the use of technology is increasing in the classroom; teachers should only be using technology (videos, computer programs, television, films) that is part of the approved curriculum; parents that feel excessive use of television or movies is taking place should notify the principal

What if the teacher tries to tell parents how to raise their child?
Listen/look for: parents have a right to raise their child as they see fit, within commonly acceptable parameters; while teachers may offer advice to parents on techniques and approaches to improve study skills, improve behavior, and resolve conflict, they are not the parents and should not attempt to tell the parents what to do with their child

What if a teacher is always out of the class and the children are unsupervised?
Listen/look for: supervision of students is a primary duty of a teacher; leaving students alone is an open door to trouble for the students, the teacher, and the school; parents that sense that a teacher is out of his classroom more than necessary should notify the principal

What happens if two teachers are arguing with each other in front of the children?
Listen/look for: squabbles between staff members have no place in a school filled with children; professionalism and common sense dictate that adults discuss disagreements in private; parents that overhear staff members arguing in front of children should notify the principal

Why Are Teachers Observed?

Nothing takes the place of actually watching a teacher in the process of teaching. The delivery of the subject's content, the teacher's interaction with the students, the reinforcement and motivation of children, and the overall organization of the teacher's presentation are all involved in a successful lesson. To know the degree of a teacher's preparation, how appropriately the lesson meets the children's needs, and the rapport with the students, a principal must see the professional in action. In some cases the teacher may know the principal is planning a visit to his or her classroom. In other cases, the teacher may not know the principal is coming. Regardless, it is very difficult for a poor teacher to become a "good" teacher just for the principal's visit. Poor teachers cannot suddenly change their teaching style, organization, and rapport with their classes. Principals know what to look for in classroom observations.

Questions to Consider

If teachers are trained to teach, why do they need to be observed?
Listen/look for: principals normally observe thousands of lessons during their tenure in administration; new approaches, innovative tech-

niques, and better ways of doing things can be discussed with teachers as part of a post-observation conference; the teaching process can be a very isolated undertaking once the classroom door is closed; principals need to continually strive to improve instruction within their buildings

Can a principal really judge a teacher's ability by observing her once or twice?

Listen/look for: formal observations are a means to an end in most schools; it is the official procedure for watching a teacher conduct a period of instruction; a teacher's ability is measured by many things in addition to the one or two official observations per year; rapport with students and parents, completion of paperwork, adherence to school rules, and reliability to carry out assigned tasks complement observations in assessing a teacher's ability to work with young people

Can a parent observe a teacher's lesson?

Listen/look for: in some cases, yes; parents interested in observing a teacher's lesson should contact the school principal; in some cases it may not be permitted because of the teacher's contract

Can't a teacher alter his teaching to please the observer?

Listen/look for: it is almost impossible for a poor teacher to suddenly discover and teach a superior lesson to impress an observer; a poor teacher seldom can deliver a high-quality presentation regardless of the circumstances

Do teachers like to be observed?

Listen/look for: some teachers become very nervous when being observed; some teachers openly invite administrators to visit their classes at any time; a small number dislike observations, considering them unnecessary and unprofessional

Why can't a principal observe teachers more often?

Listen/look for: many principals enter the profession expecting to observe teachers many times during the school year; after experiencing the many responsibilities and tasks they confront each day, many principals find there is insufficient time to do all they would like

What If the Teacher Is Doing a Poor Job?

At times, a teacher may be found to be performing below district expectations. When this occurs, the principal must begin the process of helping the teacher improve, provide resources to improve instructional techniques, or in the worse case scenario, move toward suspension or dismissal.

In schools, teachers are often isolated in individual classrooms beyond the direct supervision of principals or viewing of peers. This can create a situation where inadequate performance can arise. It is the principal's job to be watchful that all teachers, as isolated as they may be, are meeting the expectations of the district in providing a quality educational experience to all of the children in their care.

Questions to Consider

If the teacher is not teaching well, what do you do?
Listen/look for: once the ineffective teaching is discovered, the principal usually meets with the teacher in question and reviews the expectations of the district in comparison with what is happening in the classroom; normally a series of events take place including the development of written plans for remediation, scheduling of additional observations, possible involvement of peers, additional mentoring by other educators, and reevaluation of the teacher's progress toward established goals

Can the district fire a teacher that is incompetent?
Listen/look for: yes, but only after attempts have been made to improve the performance of the teacher; areas including immorality, intemperance, cruelty, persistent negligence, neglect of duties, and unsatisfactory teaching are often grounds for termination

Do other teachers ever report a poor teacher?
Listen/look for: in many cases, fellow teachers attempt to work with a weak teacher to avoid the involvement of the administration; occasionally a teacher may bring the situation to the attention of the principal, but usually the principal is already aware of the circumstances and is working to improve the situation

Do parents ever report a poor teacher?
Listen/look for: yes, parents often will contact the school if they suspect that a teacher is having a problem in class, meets their child's needs poorly, or demonstrates a lack of understanding of content material; however, many times such accusations are based on the perceptions of their child

Why can't students report a poor teacher?
Listen/look for: often children will first report what they perceive as a poor teacher to their parents, who in turn contact the principal

How long does it take to get rid of a poor teacher?
Listen/look for: dismissal of a teacher is a very serious matter because it affects the career, livelihood, and reputation of the person involved; if the teacher is tenured or has several years of experience, it may take some time for dismissal to take place; after all attempts at remediation have failed, steps can be taken to dismiss the teacher; in serious situations, poor teachers can be suspended; actual dismissal proceedings can take months

Why can't cameras be used to monitor teachers' teaching?
Listen/look for: typically teachers' contracts do not permit cameras in the classroom for the purpose of filming their lessons; many educators feel that students react differently when cameras are present; professional educators feel it is no more necessary to have cameras in their classrooms than it would be to videotape dentists, lawyers, doctors, and other professionals as they work with their clients

What techniques are used to help a poor teacher?
Listen/look for: assistance might include suggestions based on an observation, permitting a fellow teacher to observe her classes and suggest ideas, having the teacher in question observe an outstanding teacher, outside administrators observing the teacher, review of and help in preparing better lesson plans, sending the teacher to a workshop related to the classroom problem, reviewing a videotape of her lesson, and discussing ways to improve the delivery

Do schools give letters of recommendation to get rid of poor teachers?
Listen/look for: sending an inadequate teacher to another district is a poor way to handle a teaching problem; bouncing a teacher from district

to district only spreads the deficient teaching to other districts; while it may have been done in some cases in the past, it is a failure on the part of an administrator when it occurs

Can Teachers Be Fired?

In extreme cases, even when the teacher is on tenure, after remedial efforts have been exhausted a school district may take action to dismiss a teacher. This is a serious matter for the district, the school, and the employee. Care must be taken at the district level and in the school building that confidentiality be maintained and the rights of the employee be protected. If the teacher is a more experienced teacher, the friendships developed over the years may result in a division of the faculty. Some fellow teachers may believe the allegations, while others may not believe that the teacher is capable of wrongdoing.

In matters related to poor classroom performance, months of proactive work must have been completed by the administration in order for the board to consider dismissal. In incidents related to student endangerment (inappropriate touching, gross disrespect, violation of drug laws, and so on), immediate action may be called for and a teacher, or any staff member, can be suspended and referred to the board for possible dismissal.

Questions to Consider

What does it take to fire a teacher?
Listen/look for: documented indicators of inadequate teaching ability; careful and honest attempts to help the teacher improve; evidence that the teacher either chooses not to improve or cannot; careful adherence to all due process rights of the teacher; evidence of insubordination, insolence, immorality, or negligence

Doesn't tenure protect all teachers from being fired?
Listen/look for: tenure is a protection against unjustified, capricious, or arbitrary dismissal of a teacher without just cause

Why do teachers have tenure in some states?
Listen/look for: years ago, in some states, teachers were dismissed without justifiable reason, were terminated each spring and rehired

each fall to avoid salary increases, and were subject to the whims of dictatorial superintendents and unreasonable boards of education

Why do some teachers have the right to strike?
Listen/look for: in some states (Act 195 in Pennsylvania), teachers' unions have lobbied for and been successful in having legislatures enact limited right-to-strike laws; while these teachers have the right to conduct a strike if contract negotiations break down and the parties have reached an impasse, in many cases, they must return to work by a specific date to allow students to complete the required number of school days

Can a teacher be fired for immorality?
Listen/look for: yes, immorality is one of the reasons that a teacher can be dismissed; immorality charges may consist of lying and immoral acts, among others; immorality, unsatisfactory teaching, intemperance, cruelty, persistent negligence, and neglect of duties can result in dismissal

If a teacher cannot teach, why was he hired?
Listen/look for: in most incidences, it is not a case of a teacher not being able to teach, it is a question of how well he can teach; some teachers, once hired for a position, display a lack of enthusiasm for the position, fail to develop the proper rapport with students, or neglect to meet district expectations

Who Can Fire Teachers?

In many states, only a school board, or board of school directors, can dismiss a teacher. Normally, it requires a majority vote. Boards must be careful to act in a prudent manner because legal ramification may result from unfounded, inaccurate decisions or dismissals based on supposition.

In some cases, dismissal hearings may be held at open public meetings. Usually this is a choice left to the teacher in question. Typically either legal counsel or the local teachers' union represents the teacher. In every case, the district solicitor is involved to protect the district's interests, and the board sits as a panel of judges. Their decision, if it is to dismiss the staff member, is subject to appeal to the courts or, in some cases, to the state secretary of education.

Questions to Consider

If the teachers work for the principal, why can't the principal fire them?
Listen/look for: in most states a teacher actually works for the school board or the superintendent; the principal is the immediate supervisor, not the employer

Can the superintendent fire a bad teacher?
Listen/look for: certainly a superintendent can begin proceedings to dismiss or temporarily suspend a teacher; usually the school board files the charges against a teacher

Does the entire school board have to agree to fire a teacher?
Listen/look for: no, only a majority of the members of a board must vote in the affirmative to dismiss a teacher

Can a parent be involved in and give testimony at a dismissal hearing?
Listen/look for: if the district feels that a parent has creditable evidence in support of a dismissal, a parent may be called to testify

Can parental complaints help get a teacher fired?
Listen/look for: parental complaints, if verified, can be used as supportive evidence in action against a teacher

Won't the teachers' union defend the teacher being fired?
Listen/look for: teachers' unions or associations will often back a teacher to guarantee that he or she is afforded constitutional rights; additionally, if the union feels that the reasons for dismissal are unfounded, it may financially support the accused teacher through hearings and appeals; good teachers do not want poor teachers in the profession

What If Parents Disagree with What the Teacher Is Doing?

In many cases, the judgment of a teacher's performance is seen through the eyes of a child because the parent is not present in the classroom. Parents listen to their child and form opinions, sometimes based on bias and youthful perspectives. In some cases, these reports by children may be colored by recent disciplinary action taken by the teacher, poor test results, or childish schemes intent on hurting a specific teacher. While children must be protected, parents are warned to be aware that children sometimes see things differently than adults. The teacher seen as mean by students may be a good disciplinarian. The teacher seen as picking on students may be assigning more homework than other teachers are. In short, a child's perspective must be open to question until collaborating information is forthcoming.

Questions to Consider

What if a teacher is harassing a child?
Listen/look for: teachers are not permitted to harass any child; teachers found guilty of such behavior may be disciplined

What if a teacher is unfair to a child?
Listen/look for: teachers are to operate their classes in a fair and unbiased manner; caution must be given that many children feel a teacher is unfair if they do not receive the grades they feel they deserve; certainly, teachers should be capable of justifying grades and treatment of children if questioned

If a student does not make the cheerleading squad or a sports team, how can the parents appeal the decision?
Listen/look for: making a sports team depends on many factors including the competition, the number of spots open, and the skill level of the person trying out for the team; usually coaches are looking for the most capable students for their teams; parents may choose to meet with the coach, but usually it is very difficult to alter team membership after tryouts have been completed

What if a teacher has unjust rules in his classroom?
Listen/look for: normally classroom rules support and augment schoolwide rules; classroom rules usually relate to acceptable behavior in the classroom; many principals are aware of their teachers' rules and if they appear to be unjust will suggest alternatives

If a student's coach conducts unreasonable practice sessions, what can parents do?
Listen/look for: a meeting with the coach will often clarify the goals of the practices; if practices continue to be viewed as unreasonable or harsh, the parent should contact the school principal or athletic director

If a teacher lies to a student, how can parents respect her?
Listen/look for: lying, in any form, has no place in a school; teachers that deliberately lie to students should apologize and make certain it does not happen in the future; it is easy for a person to lose respect and very difficult to gain it back

If a teacher is rude to a student, how do parents get him to apologize?
Listen/look for: teachers are usually gracious enough to apologize when they have been rude or thoughtless

What if a teacher is rude and disrespectful to her classes?
Listen/look for: there is no excuse for a teacher being rude to students; principals aware of teacher rudeness will typically attempt to work with the teacher to help her become more tolerant

What if a teacher is presenting incorrect information to the class?
Listen/look for: parents that become aware that a teacher is delivering incorrect material in classes should notify the principal; principals will check the content of material presented in classes

What if homework is excessive?
Listen/look for: excessive or insufficient homework has been a discussion point for many years; often what is seen as excessive homework is the result of students putting off assignments until they accumulate large workloads; parents should discuss the amount of homework with the principal if it seems to be excessive or too limited

What if the teacher dislikes a child?
Listen/look for: few teachers dislike children; teachers may feel a student is disruptive or has a behavior problem, but they normally dislike the behavior not the child

Aren't some teachers absent a lot?

Listen/look for: most teachers' contracts permit a certain number of sick days per year; in some cases these sick days can accumulate from year to year; unless a teacher is violating the sick leave clause or is lying about being sick, the district will normally permit legal absences

Why do teachers always complain about stress?

Listen/look for: some teachers feel that many of their responsibilities contribute to feelings of frustration and stress; most teachers are with students almost continually the entire day; often there is little time to relax, go to the restroom, or get a drink of water; teachers are under increasing pressure to increase student test scores; some have extra duties such as bus monitor, hall monitor, cafeteria supervisor, or restroom monitor in addition to their hectic teaching schedules; most take work home at night to grade or review, and through it all, they are expected to smile, be pleasant, and take a personal interest in every child

What if the teacher is uncooperative with parents?

Listen/look for: part of a teacher's responsibility is to work with and be respectful of parents; teachers that show disrespect toward parents or are uncooperative in working toward worthwhile goals for children should be reported to the principal

What if a parent objects to the actions of a teacher while out of school?

Listen/look for: teachers that display behavior that goes against community values or interests may be subject to reprimand at school; grossly offensive behavior should be reported to the principal

How Does a Parent Know If the Teacher Is Teaching the Right Thing?

Sometimes, children bring home stories about their classes. At times these stories may be based on their understanding of the information presented in the class. If teachers are presenting incorrect or inaccurate material to students, it must be corrected. If, on the other hand, students are misconstruing information taught, the student should be corrected.

The subject curriculum is the approved material for instructional purposes. The board has reviewed and approved the adoption and implementation of the curriculum, texts, and supplemental material (to some degree) in all classes. While teachers certainly have the freedom to present the material according to their individual styles, the basic material presented must be accurate, free from editorial comment, and unbiased. The teacher's position must never be a place for an individual to promote or advocate opinions counter to community mores, counter to district approval, or extreme in nature.

Questions to Consider

If a parent questions a teacher's methods, whom does he contact?
Listen/look for: normally a conference with the teacher is the first step; if the parent is unsatisfied with the teacher's response, the principal should be contacted

Won't the teacher pick on a child if his parents report the teacher for doing something wrong?
Listen/look for: in fact much to the contrary; most teachers tend to increase their attentiveness toward students if their parents have filed a complaint; if a teacher is suspected of mistreating a student because of his parents, the principal should be informed at once

If parents find other students to support their child's accusations, can they get action?
Listen/look for: the best plan is to present the information to the principal, along with the names of collaborating witnesses, and he will pursue the matter; often students will modify their testimonies when questioned by the principal

If a parent thinks the teacher is biased in her presentation of   (subject)   , can the parent report it to the principal?
Listen/look for: yes, bias has no place in a school; many times it is the perception of the student rather than true bias on the part of the teacher

THE CLASSROOM

A teacher's classroom can be a very isolated place to work. Separated from other teachers by the classroom walls, a teacher works independently much of the time. When instituted, team teaching, co-teaching, or turn teaching can sometimes help avoid the isolation of a self-contained classroom.

Teachers are normally well versed in the curriculum approved by the school board and their responsibilities related to teaching their subjects or grade levels. In some schools teachers plan and organize lessons as part of a team or department. This allows new teachers to better understand the system and the scope and sequence of their curricular area. In such team planning sessions, teachers can voice concerns, discuss approaches to various topics, and coordinate group presentations. It is an excellent opportunity for the team or department to streamline their lessons and guard against overextension in one particular area.

Attempts should be made to make each classroom reflect the subject taught. Many teachers try to make their classrooms as comfortable as possible with plants, artwork, and pleasant surroundings that enhance a relaxed learning environment.

There is no doubt that some lessons are better prepared and presented than others. Lessons depend on several factors, so differences always exist. The training and experience of the teacher, the supplies and facilities available, and the content of the lesson itself affect the delivery of the material in a presentation. Principals normally check lesson plans to gauge the preparation for lessons; occasional observations of teachers' lessons are also helpful. In many schools a watchful eye on the scores recorded on standardized tests also serves as a measure of lessons presented and material learned by students.

If parents have questions related to the material presented by teachers, the information printed in texts, or the quality of delivery within a teacher's course, they should consult the building principal. If deficiencies are discovered it is reasonable for the parent to request corrective action.

Questions to Consider

Does the principal review the teachers' weekly lesson plans?
Listen/look for: in most schools, principals periodically review teachers' lesson plans; often a department or grade level is scrutinized at various times throughout the year

How does a principal know the quality of each teacher's lesson?
Listen/look for: the quality of a lesson usually cannot be determined through review of lesson plans; to understand and assess the quality of lessons an investigation of exams and tests needs to be undertaken; review of student test papers provides evidence of material taught and mastered

How does the principal know what a teacher is really teaching?
Listen/look for: through review of lesson plans, informal and formal observations, review of test scores, and analysis of teacher-prepared tests

Are test results reviewed to see that the teacher is presenting the approved curriculum?
Listen/look for: yes, tests are periodically reviewed to assess the content of lessons

How Can an Elementary Teacher Know All the Subjects?

Teaching children at the elementary level typically requires basic knowledge in many areas. However, the degree of depth and scope of the subject area is normally less comprehensive than it is at the middle or high school levels. Elementary teachers must be adequately trained to provide basic information to children appropriate to their developmental age. This entails reading development, basic math instruction, introduction to science, enhanced knowledge of social studies, and other areas on which secondary education can build. While some elementary teachers may have specialties in areas such as reading or math, they usually are required to teach all subjects at the elementary level. An exception exists in schools where there is some degree of departmentalization.

Questions to Consider

How can a single teacher know all about math, reading, geography, and so on?

Listen/look for: elementary teachers are well versed in the various subject areas they teach; colleges cover the basic content of subjects such as math, social studies, geography, language arts, and science; teachers usually major in a specific area and often have a minor in another area of interest; principals often rely on these majors if departmentalization is implemented

Can an elementary teacher teach physical education, art, and music?

Listen/look for: yes, elementary teaching certificates usually include physical education, art, and music

Are elementary teachers trained to meet the needs of academically advanced children?

Listen/look for: teachers are trained to seek out and work with children that display gifted abilities in their classes; while some schools have specially trained teachers for gifted children, all teachers help promote giftedness

Don't all teachers receive the same training?

Listen/look for: at the elementary level most teachers receive similar training in the basics of teaching; at the secondary level, teachers are schooled in specific subject areas that eventually become their areas of certification

Do teachers really want to teach the slow learners?

Listen/look for: many teachers not only enjoy teaching developmentally delayed children but volunteer to do so; there is something gratifying in helping a youngster, who previously was experiencing problems in school, achieve success

How many subjects does an elementary teacher teach in one day?

Listen/look for: often an elementary teacher may teach language arts (reading), math, social studies, and science; additionally study skills, geography, handwriting, spelling, and other subjects are often taught

How Much Time Is Spent in Lecturing?

Each teacher develops a style in his or her approach to teaching. While some teachers may spend the first part of a period presenting new material through a type of lecture, others may prefer to involve the children in activities designed to permit discovery of new concepts. Normally it is not recommended that extensive lecturing be used as the primary means of presentation at the elementary level. The attention span, the need for hands-on activities, and the depth of the content within courses mandate that teachers structure their lessons appropriately to meet the demands of younger children.

Questions to Consider

Do your teachers lecture most of the time?
Listen/look for: in many schools teachers use limited lecturing; certainly new material or new concepts may need to be introduced through lectures, but most teachers recognize that children learn best through hands-on practice

What methods other than lecturing are used to teach children?
Listen/look for: team teaching, role playing, small group work, cooperative learning, student presentations, computer-based instruction, videos, and field trips are some of the approaches used in many classes

If a child takes notes poorly, how can he learn from a lecture?
Listen/look for: note taking is a valuable skill; normally teachers will assist students experiencing difficulty with note taking

TEACHING TECHNIQUES

The vast array of approaches used in classrooms is almost limitless. Some teachers may utilize technology, while others rely on hands-on experimentation. Others may involve student role-playing, while some may use cooperative learning activities for instruction. Regardless of the techniques used, the teacher should relate the type of student activity to the area being studied. While math lessons might be more appropriately taught using computers and spreadsheets, a social studies lesson might be a wonderful subject to employ role-playing. Parents should ask their child's teacher what approaches he or she uses as part of the lessons.

Questions to Consider

Are relevant videos used in the classrooms?
Listen/look for: yes, videos and films related to the curriculum are used as supplements

Can a child record the teacher's lectures?
Listen/look for: under normal circumstances, recording of lectures is not encouraged; if special circumstances exist, a child may be permitted to record lectures with the teacher's permission

Are students encouraged to ask questions?
Listen/look for: yes, many educators believe asking questions is the key to learning; questions are necessary to clarify statements, ideas, and concepts

What Is a Typical Lesson Format?

As stated earlier, lessons come in all shapes and sizes. Often a lesson begins by restating concepts from the previous day. This introduction serves as a bridge for the current day's lesson. Teachers try to involve the students' experience related to the lesson. They use motivational techniques to reinforce positive responses and creative approaches to present the new information. Good teachers continually engage their students in active participation. They encourage, remind, and build bridges of understanding so that every child comprehends the day's concepts. At the conclusion of most classes the teacher summarizes the lessons learned or the terms, concepts, or information taught and lays out the plans for the following day. Lessons should be concluded, as one might tie up a package, and presented to the students for their benefit.

Few lessons stand alone. Teachers try to show the connection between lessons by summarizing A, B, and C that were taught today and their relationship to D, E, and F that will be taught tomorrow. Or teachers may work with their colleagues and show the association between, perhaps, math and science or English and social studies. This helps students realize that a natural, shared correlation exists across curricular areas.

Questions to Consider

What is a typical lesson format?
Listen/look for: classes usually begin with the teacher introducing the lesson for the day; often a quick review of the previous day is presented, new material is presented, students are engaged in some activity, and a summary of the lesson is presented

Do children have to remain quiet during the class?
Listen/look for: in most classes students are energetically engaged in meaningful activity; to the casual observer this activity may seem unorganized and noisy; most teachers and principals recognize working noise as opposed to unnecessary noise

Are students allowed to get up and move during the class?
Listen/look for: student movement during class depends on the type of lesson; in many classes, after the curricular material is presented, students become engaged in activities that permit movement within the classroom

Does a child have to pledge the flag?
Listen/look for: no; the U.S. Supreme Court ruled in 1943 that students do not have to participate in saying the pledge to the flag; students are expected to remain quiet and not disrupt the pledge for others

Do teachers ever work together across curricular areas?
Listen/look for: yes, it is common for teachers to coordinate their lessons; team planning and interdisciplinary teaching is common in many schools

How are students motivated?
Listen/look for: motivation is an internal drive; teachers can help students to become more motivated by providing an enriching environment, exciting lessons, interesting discussions, and recognition for work well done

Can students begin homework in class?

Listen/look for: many teachers permit students to start their homework the last few minutes of class to allow them to clarify any misunderstanding and to assist those needing more help

Are There Distractions and Interruptions during the Lesson?

A calm and nondisruptive environment is crucial to uninterrupted instruction and student learning. The reduction or elimination of bells, public address announcements, and other interruptions during instructional periods is a major help in providing lesson continuity and reducing student distractions.

While structure is needed in all schools, the excessive use of bells to change classes, public address announcements to communicate with staff and students, time taken to discipline students, and unlimited access to classrooms while teachers are teaching can greatly interfere with student learning.

Questions to Consider

How often are classes interrupted by public address announcements?

Listen/look for: announcements should be made only when necessary; in many schools, after morning announcements the public address system is not used during the day; many teachers feel that it takes up to five minutes to return students to task after being interrupted by an announcement

How often do the bells ring?

Listen/look for: in many schools bell schedules are reduced to as few times per day as possible; once instituted, many schools find that teachers do not need bells to signal change of classes

Can students come and go, in and out of classes?

Listen/look for: accountability is a major concern of school personnel; students are permitted to leave classes for valid reasons; going to the restroom or the health room are normally permitted

Don't discipline problems interrupt the teacher's lesson?
Listen/look for: occasionally a misbehaving student will interrupt a lesson; experienced teachers know how to deal with such disruptions without seriously interfering with other students; undoubtedly, if a classroom contains students that regularly misbehave and cause a commotion it needs to be rectified

How Important Is Class Size?

Discussions over class size have been going on for many years. Some educators quote studies indicating that smaller classes in the primary grades have a positive influence on achievement. Others argue that while some influence is noted in grades one through three, no specific advantage is sustained beyond the primary grades. At the same time, many parents look back on their days in school, saying, "We had classes of forty when I was in school; what is the problem with thirty kids in a room now?" But today's schools comprise elements that make class size an important consideration. Students diagnosed with ADHD, learning support (LS), and other special education identifications in regular classes tax the teacher's ability to work with large groups. The introduction of computers and other technology increases the need for extra space in classrooms. Recent emphasis on test results have worried teachers that large numbers of students can have a dramatic, negative effect on the test scores.

Questions to Consider

Isn't class size just an excuse for teachers that want it easy?
Listen/look for: many educators feel that class size has a direct effect on the quality of instruction; many teachers feel that fewer students in a classroom reduce the number of interruptions for disciplinary reasons and permit individual work with students; as more and more attention is devoted to individualizing instruction, teachers want class sizes that permit more opportunity to work one-on-one with students

What is the problem with classes over thirty-five?
Listen/look for: many would argue larger classes mean more discipline problems, more talking, more movement, more noise, less room, less working area, less room for computers, more interruptions, less one-

on-one work, and less rapport between the teacher and the students; parents need to ask themselves, are five children more difficult to raise than two; the quality of the teacher is the key factor

Do larger classes really have more discipline problems?
Listen/look for: many feel that increased class size results in a proportional increase in the number of disciplinary incidents

Does a child get the help he needs in a large class?
Listen/look for: teachers try very hard to provide the help students need regardless of the class size, but with a certain number of minutes in each period and only one teacher available, increases in the number of students usually mean less time to work with each student individually

How large are the classes in this school?
Listen/look for: class sizes vary across schools; in the primary grades smaller classes are desired because students are learning the basics necessary for future success in school: reading, writing, spelling, and so on; in all classes, the number of students in attendance has an effect on the ability of the teacher to work one-on-one with individual students

What is the ratio between boys and girls in this school?
Listen/look for: the school has little control over the number of boys and girls that are enrolled; attempts are made to balance classes; attempts are made to reflect the overall ratio between girls and boys in as many classes as possible

How Are Students Grouped in the School?

Students are often scheduled into various groupings in school. Everyone is familiar with the grade level groupings and division of students into subject areas for instruction. Particularly at the elementary level, students may also be grouped based on their developmental level. In many schools special groups are made for reading and math to accommodate those students that may have difficulty comprehending regular instruction or may need more challenging work assigned. Some teachers find grouping together students of like ability adds to a better pace in instruction and the ability to adapt the curriculum to the learning needs of the students in the particular group. Likewise, learning disability classes, gifted classes, and remedial classes may be formed to focus the instruction on the individuals at that level.

Some educators disagree with grouping of students into various subgroups. They feel there may be a loss of role models within a class if the better academic students are removed. Furthermore, the grouping together of children having academic difficulties could result in larger numbers of discipline problems in a class.

Regardless of the existence of groupings, students often group themselves. Selection of courses of study and electives at the secondary level tend to track students into groups.

Questions to Consider

What is homogeneous grouping?
Listen/look for: homogeneous grouping places students of like ability in classes together; examples of homogeneous grouping include accelerated reading classes, remedial reading classes, gifted programs, college prep classes, and some special education classes

What is heterogeneous grouping?
Listen/look for: heterogeneous grouping places students with dissimilar abilities in classes together; examples of heterogeneous grouping include general math classes, gym classes, general science classes, and basic English classes

What is the best grouping?
Listen/look for: differences of opinion exist regarding the best grouping; some educators feel that homogeneous grouping allows the teacher to work with the particular abilities of the class, helping the slow learners better and enriching the higher achieving students more easily; advocates of heterogeneous grouping point out that placing students with select groups of their peers eliminates role models for the slower students and creates a clique for the advanced students

What if a parent wants a homogenous grouping for her gifted child?
Listen/look for: many schools offer advanced classes or gifted classes for those students that meet the criteria (perhaps a 130-plus IQ) and still group most children in heterogeneous groups

Is cooperative learning allowed in the classes?
Listen/look for: in many classes teachers form small groups and, after instruction, allow the children to work in cooperative learning groups; forming small groups where each member of the group has responsibility for an aspect of the task helps set the stage for teamwork later in life

Do students have final exams each year?
Listen/look for: schools vary in their use of final exams; some states require final exams as part of the local and state assessment; often it depends on the subject and grade level of the students

Is competition between students a good strategy?
Listen/look for: competition is part of life; even if the teacher tried to avoid competition, students would create contests among themselves

Are guest speakers used in classes?
Listen/look for: guest speakers are often used in classes; with the costs of field trips going up each year, it is much less expensive to bring in an expert on a subject than pay for the transportation of children to visit a site

Are Field Trips Necessary?

The opportunity to leave school and travel to educational sites is often helpful in understanding topics under study. While a field trip to some may seem like a day off school, it is exactly the opposite. Teachers spend a considerable amount of extra time setting up agendas, scheduling buses, arranging for lunches, preparing the students for the trip, and incorporating the trip into their lessons. In many teachers' minds, a field trip is much more demanding than a normal day in school.

Field trips on school time should be related to the curriculum. They should enhance, reinforce, supplement, and enrich the classroom lessons. What is more appropriate than visiting a zoo if animal study is the topic, traveling to a science center to see examples of modern technology, or actually experiencing the wonders of nature in a woodland setting? Field trips can serve as a valuable instructional tool for teachers.

Questions to Consider

Why are field trips needed?

Listen/look for: field trips help broaden the learning experiences of many children; some things cannot be presented in the classroom as well as they can be at specific sites (zoos, historic locations, science exhibits); however, as costs go up, many schools have had to reduce the number of authorized field trips

Isn't a field trip just a day off school for teachers?

Listen/look for: anyone that has attempted to supervise twenty-five or thirty children as they meander through a zoo or museum realizes that a field trip is anything but an easy day for a teacher

What if a child becomes ill while on a field trip?

Listen/look for: teachers are trained to respond to student illnesses at all times; cell phones are usually carried by teachers, and the school can be contacted in the event of any emergency; in cases of a serious nature, teachers may often act in loco parentis for the welfare of the child

Can parents volunteer to go on a field trip?

Listen/look for: often teachers are happy to have parents accompany them on field trips to assist with supervision; parents need to realize that going on a field trip is different than taking their child on a trip; there are normally certain responsibilities that parents must assume when serving as a field trip helper

Don't parents pay for the teachers to teach, not to go on trips?

Listen/look for: going on field trips is teaching; normally teachers spend time in class explaining what the students will be seeing on the trip and how it relates to the curriculum; on returning from a field trip, teachers usually spend time reviewing the sights seen and how they supplement the regular studies

What about Field Trips and Safety?

Once a child leaves the protection of the school building different possibilities exist that could affect his or her safety. Travel to and from the school during field trips incurs the possibility of traffic accidents.

No one can guarantee what another careless driver might do. Once at the site of the field trip, both teachers and students are in unfamiliar territory. Is the property clean and well maintained? Are chairs, stairs, and facilities regularly inspected for safety reasons? Who monitors the other visitors at the field trip site? Is the student–teacher ratio such that proper supervision is possible and every student is within close proximity to a professional staff member?

Where will the children be eating lunch? Is the food service monitored as it is in the school lunchroom? Is contact information available to permit the notification of parents in the event of a child's illness or injury? Can the school contact the supervisors of the field trip if there is a problem with weather, a problem with bus pick-up, or an emergency? Many questions exist. However, a well-organized school principal and competent staff should be aware of the potential risks involved in all field trips and take steps to alleviate both the parents' concerns and the possible risks.

Questions to Consider

Do field trip supervisors carry cell phones during the trip?
Listen/look for: contact with teachers while on field trips is important; cell phones are carried by all teachers on every field trip; a contact person is available at every location visited by students on a field trip; teachers are to contact the school periodically while on a field trip

Who selects the location to visit on a field trip?
Listen/look for: normally teachers are the primary initiators of field trips; often field trips are related to curricular areas; at times department chairpersons recommend field trips that supplement or enhance the curriculum; principals and parents may sometimes recommend sites of interest for field trips

Can a parent refuse to allow his child to go on a field trip?
Listen/look for: in most cases field trips are closely related to the approved curriculum and are preapproved by the school board; students may, under certain circumstances, be excused from participation in specific field trips; as part of the teaching process, field trips serve a valuable purpose, and therefore missing field trips results in lost instruction

Who administers medication to students while on a field trip?

Listen/look for: in some cases field trips consume only part of the school day; in cases where a child will be away from school at the time scheduled for medication, a reliable adult will administer medication; parents are sometimes invited to go on the field trip and administer medication to their child

Are there procedures to follow in the event of an emergency during a field trip?

Listen/look for: professional educators know the procedures to follow in the event of an emergency while on a field trip; in the event of an emergency staff members are to contact the school, the police, or emergency resources at once; in most cases the school would then contact parents

What is the normal ratio between students and staff members on trips?

Listen/look for: the ratio between students and staff members varies depending on the type and length of the field trip; usually a ratio of about five to one is considered adequate; in some cases larger ratios are acceptable if the trip consists of large group presentations

How is lunch handled on a field trip?

Listen/look for: lunch may be either brown bag, school supplied, or purchased en route; parents are notified of the nature of the trip and the need for a packed lunch or extra money for purchasing meals

Who pays for field trips?

Listen/look for: normally field trips are funded as part of the school budget; in some districts a small fee may be charged for students to attend certain field trips to offset costs; sometimes fund-raisers are conducted to finance student field trips; PTAs often sponsor field trips as part of their effort to support the school and enhance student learning

Are field trips part of the curriculum?

Listen/look for: in most cases field trips are part of the curriculum; in some cases field trips are activity oriented (sports teams, club trips, class celebrations, senior trips)

CHAPTER 5

The Student

STUDENT BEHAVIOR

Rules are the basic elements that keep a school operating in an acceptable manner. Rules create consistent standards within the school that help promote appropriate behavior. Common sense and the compliance to social norms, in addition to cooperation with school staff members, lead to a good learning environment.

In an attempt to communicate school rules and regulations, most schools publish student handbooks. Careful reading of this handbook can often explain most of the rules under which a school operates. Additionally, most school rules are derived from district policy.

The classroom teacher is on the front line of enforcement. This professional educator, knowledgeable of the developmental levels of students, the rationale behind rules, and the appropriate manner to deal with infractions, is in the best position to carry out school rule implementation.

Principals are eager to discuss and clarify school rules with parents. No one, including the principal, wants students to violate established rules, resulting in disciplinary action. Besides, teachers and principals know that without the parents' assistance, student adherence to school rules is much more difficult. Once again, it is a team effort. Rules are created to set consistent standards within the school, promote common-sense compliance to social norms, and encourage cooperation with school staff members. To be effective, rules must be developed by individuals knowledgeable about student developmental levels, administered by principals and teachers in fair and unbiased ways, and enforced through reasonable, relevant punishment.

Students must be told of the rules often. They need to be reminded why rules exist and of the advantage of their enforcement to the student body. Students must understand that without rules against bullying, harassment, and fighting, their rights may be violated and they may become victims. Rules exist for the good of the whole.

Questions to Consider

Can a parent review the school rules related to ___subject___?
Listen/look for: parents are always welcome to review school rules; many school rules are outlined in the student handbook; student rights and responsibilities are open for both student and parent review

How does the rule on ___subject___ help students learn?
Listen/look for: rules are written for the common good; while some rules may not be to the liking of all students, they are needed for the protection of the school population; school rules, like laws in regular society, should be reasonable and fair; the school rules are fairly written and consistently enforced

Some students violate school rules. Why doesn't the principal stop them?
Listen/look for: teachers and administrators enforce rules whenever they are aware of them being violated; if a parent knows of a violation taking place, school officials appreciate being made aware of the situation; principals can only discipline students for violations of school rules when they are aware of the infractions

If a parent disagrees with a specific rule, how can he challenge it?
Listen/look for: parents have the right to challenge any rule; parents that feel a rule is a violation of student rights should consult with the building principal; if the parent is still not satisfied with the decision of the principal he can appeal to the superintendent

Do the parents and students have input into the creation of rules?
Listen/look for: normally, school rules are written with input from teachers and principals; parents may request membership on disciplinary committees or policy committees to help formulate rules and regulations; sometimes students at the high school level have opportunity to suggest changes in school rules

What happens if two students are fighting but one started it?
Listen/look for: determining who started a fight can be difficult; after investigation of the incident principals determine the degree of guilt of each party and administer discipline; if the degree of guilt varies, the consequences often are more harsh for the individual that started the altercation

What gives the principal the right to enforce a rule parents disagree with?
Listen/look for: school rules, like laws, can be challenged in the proper manner; school rules, like laws, can be overturned if found to be unjust; school rules, like laws, must be followed until they are altered or rescinded

Why can't a child wear her new fashionable hat in the school?
Listen/look for: wearing a hat, in most schools, is considered a distraction and disruptive to the educational process; students need to learn that there is a time and place for wearing hats, and inside the school is not appropriate

Does a staff member have to see a child misbehave to punish him?
Listen/look for: certainly it is best if an adult sees a child violate a rule; however, the testimony of a creditable witness must be considered relevant; usually substantiation of a witness's claims is needed for action to be taken

Why are some students believed and not others?
Listen/look for: many times it is not a question of believing one child over another; sometimes the strong, substantiated testimony of several students points to the guilty party; principals also look at a student's past record and consider if a pattern of behavior is present

Before a principal renders a decision concerning the punishment, will they listen to a child's side of the story?
Listen/look for: principals attempt to listen to and consider the testimony of all parties involved in an incident; fairness demands that all parties have the opportunity to tell their side of the story

Do teachers ever punish the entire class if a few students misbehave?
Listen/look for: group punishment is never a good idea; in every class or large group, there are individual students that are completely innocent; to punish an entire class because of the actions of a few is not only unfair, it is also poor discipline

Where does a parent go to appeal a principal's decision?
Listen/look for: normally an appeal of a principal's decision should go to her immediate supervisor or possibly the superintendent; before taking an appeal to a higher level, it is the obligation of the parent to meet with the principal and discuss the incident

How is a punishment going to affect a child's education?
Listen/look for: it is hoped that the discipline that follows a violation will be a learning opportunity for the student involved; in many cases work missed can be made up; violations of school rules are kept in the student's records for the current academic year only (exceptions may include drug-related incidents, weapon violations, and alcohol violations)

Do principals talk to students to verify a child's defense?
Listen/look for: in most cases students may request that their side of the story be collaborated by witnesses; in incidents where a teacher or principal actually witnessed the violation (hitting a student, running in the hallway, being disrespectful to a teacher), bringing in other students does not alter the fact that the violation was seen by a responsible adult

Do accusers need to have collaborating witnesses?
Listen/look for: taking one child's word over another's is difficult to defend; normally it is best to have collaborating witnesses to verify the facts in a case

When will punishments be assigned?
Listen/look for: most school officials feel that the assignment and serving of a punishment immediately after the violation is best; in some incidents, it is necessary to notify parents or wait until the potential appeals are complete before punishment can be administered

What Happens to Students That Bully Others?

The statement that bullying is merely a matter of "boys will be boys" flies in the face of today's thinking. Educators know that being picked on not only causes depression and feelings of rejection but also may lead to retaliation and a "getting even" mentality. There is never a good reason to harass, pick on, tease, or bully others. Students committing such violations of school policy often suffer from low self-esteem and strike out at others to cover their own inadequate self-worth. No, bullying is not "boys will be boys"; it is a psychological or physical attack on another.

Bullying has become a major concern in schools because it often leads to additional aggression and violence. Principals attempt to discover the person responsible for bullying, but they sometimes encounter a problem. When two students come to the principal's office, each typically has a story to tell. Each blames the other for the bullying. Both students often have witnesses that defend their positions and collaborate their side of the story. The problem is, whom should the principal believe? Here the experienced principal will call on his or her knowledge of student behavior, look at past records of misbehavior, and consult teachers that may know the students better. Finally, a conclusion is reached and the principal, finding the majority of supportive evidence on one side or the other, renders a decision. Warnings are given, staff is requested to monitor the two individuals, and if additional incidents of bullying occur, further action will be called for.

Questions to Consider

If a child harasses another child, what will be done?
Listen/look for: once a charge of harassment is made the principal is obligated to investigate the matter; just because a parent (not present when the alleged incident took place) makes a charge does not mean it has substance; after a thorough investigation of the facts in the case, a decision will be rendered

If a child tells another student, "I'm going to kill you," what can a parent do?
Listen/look for: matters that relate to the safety of students should be brought to the attention of the principal at once; if the principal does not investigate the matter, the parent should consult the immediate supervisor or superintendent

If a child is receiving harassing phone calls at home, can the school stop them?
Listen/look for: school officials have no jurisdiction over phone calls made outside of school; parents should contact local telephone companies or the police

Can a parent have the names and phone numbers of students bullying his child?

Listen/look for: school officials are not permitted to release the names and phone numbers of any students or parents; in some cases the school principal will call the other parent and suggest that he contact the concerned parent; additionally, the principal will follow up on any bullying allegations

Can a principal stop a group of students that are teasing another student?

Listen/look for: excessive teasing is a form of harassment and has no place in a school; principals and guidance counselors will typically work with the students involved to eliminate the teasing

Is there a school rule or district policy about bullying?

Listen/look for: yes, almost all schools have rules forbidding bullying of others

Are bullies referred to the guidance teacher for counseling?

Listen/look for: guidance counselors routinely work with students displaying antisocial or disruptive behavior; confidentiality rules forbid the discussion of other children

Can a boy physically defend himself if he is bullied?

Listen/look for: in the school setting students are surrounded by teachers and other adults; as such, there normally is no need to physically defend oneself; some principals tell students to report bullying to an adult and only resort to physical action if they are in a place where adult help cannot be found

Why does it take so long to take action against an accused bully?

Listen/look for: sometimes school action seems to move slowly; parents need to be reminded that school officials need to afford all students due process, contact and meet with parents, and provide time for adequate investigation

Do teachers monitor student behavior and potential bullying situations?

Listen/look for: teachers are normally requested to step into the hallways between classes; locker areas, gyms, lobbies, auditoriums, and other areas are routinely patrolled

Are There Student Gangs in the School?

Gang activity is prevalent in some schools. In other (primarily rural) schools they are less evident. Graffiti, gang colors being worn, gang slogans, and other evidence of gang activity are signs that a school must immediately take action to control the situation. Police are often called in to discuss gang issues with staff members, parents are involved in the sharing of information, and plans are made to monitor and regulate organized activity in the school.

Most often, gangs operate outside the school's jurisdiction. Because of this, it is typically impossible for the school to alter actual gang affiliations. Gangs represent a community-wide problem, and the school can only cooperate and help the entire community deal with the issue.

Questions to Consider

Are there signs of gang activity in the school?
Listen/look for: the signs of gang activity are seldom seen in the school; use of the dress code has reduced the wearing of gang-related clothing; if painted symbols of gang activities are found they are removed as soon as possible

Are teachers trained to spot gang signs, slogans, and words?
Listen/look for: police often educate staff members about gang-related signs, slogans, and words to watch for in their classes

Is there gang-related graffiti found in the school?
Listen/look for: graffiti is removed as soon as it is found; the school tries to keep gang-related paintings and drawings out of the school environment through fair but strict rules and consequences

Are students permitted to wear gang-related clothing?
Listen/look for: known gang-related clothing is not allowed in the school because it is disruptive to the educational process

Why doesn't the principal require uniforms to help break up the gangs?
Listen/look for: the establishment of a school dress code or uniforms is a matter for the school board; parents that wish the initiation of a student dress code should contact the school board or superintendent

Does the school have policies related to gang organizations?

Listen/look for: in many communities gangs are part of the neighborhoods around the schools; schools attempt to keep gang-related activities out of the schoolhouse

Are the local police working with the school on gang-related issues?

Listen/look for: police normally communicate with school officials regarding gang activities near the school; police often provide updates to faculty on gang signs and symbols so that teachers can become better partners in reducing gang activity

Is the school property safe from gang activities after school hours?

Listen/look for: few schools can state unequivocally that gang activity does not take place around their schools; many schools take steps to guard school property against gang activity, and in many cases, gangs choose to meet elsewhere

Do staff members monitor school property before and after school to protect children from gang activities?

Listen/look for: teachers are normally hired to teach; security guards are hired to patrol and secure school property; naturally, if teachers or principals see inappropriate activity taking place they have an obligation to report it to police

What programs exist that address gang-related issues?

Listen/look for: some schools bring in police to discuss gang-related issues with staff members; principals may attend conferences on gangs in their areas; school districts may provide in-service training for teachers

Are students engaged in gang-related activities disciplined?

Listen/look for: if the gang activity interferes with the educational process or directly jeopardizes the safety of students the school will take action

What If a Child Is Falsely Accused?

Principals base their decisions on the facts as they understand them. After thoroughly investigating the circumstances surrounding an incident, principals reach a conclusion and make their decisions. While it is certainly possible that the principal may make a mistake because of faulty data, experience has shown that once a conclusion is reached, a decision should be made. Parents surely have the right to disagree with any decision, but they should do so in a respectful manner and with the realization that principals normally render their decisions based on facts, without prejudice or bias.

Questions to Consider

Hasn't there always been bullying and fighting at school?
Listen/look for: yes, bullying and fighting have been a part of school life for many years, but that does not mean it should be condoned; recent acts of violence in schools clearly indicate that bullying and fighting sometimes result in more serious violent actions; most parents would agree it is best to resolve conflict nonviolently

How strictly are rules enforced?
Listen/look for: to be effective, rules should be fairly written and consistently enforced; while there sometimes are extenuating circumstances, making exceptions usually results in inconsistencies, lack of trust in school officials, and eroding of the rule

Are there ever any exceptions made for extenuating circumstances?
Listen/look for: many school principals are aware of personal matters that could have an effect on their decisions regarding punishment; students involved in behavior related to a disability, for example, may have alternative punishments assigned

Why is bullying such a big deal in schools?
Listen/look for: recent incidents, including the shootings at Columbine, have reminded school principals of the need to monitor and intervene between students that are experiencing conflict, harassment, or other actions that could cause a violent reaction; most teachers and principals feel it is part of the school's role to help students settle disagreements

Do girls ever bully each other?
Listen/look for: yes, girls can often be involved in teasing others; often girls form groups that attempt to shun or show disrespect to other girls; bullying by anyone is wrong

What can a parent do to stop bullying?
Listen/look for: remind children that teasing and bullying others is always wrong; help them realize that when they stand by and let classmates tease and embarrass others they become part of the problem

Doesn't a child have a right to defend himself?
Listen/look for: if a student is alone in an isolated alley or attacked when he is beyond adult help, he should certainly fight off the attacker; in schools, adults are normally only a few yards away and can be reached for assistance

Why is a dress code necessary?
Listen/look for: many school officials believe that a uniform dress code reduces gang-related clothing in the school; some school principals feel that a dress code helps avoid the clothing discrepancy between students of various income levels; clothing must not interfere with the safety of students

If there is a rumor that a teacher is very mean to her classes, what can be done?
Listen/look for: rumors are often incorrect or exaggerated; students sometimes consider teachers mean if they are perceived as assigning extensive homework; teachers that are strong disciplinarians are sometimes viewed as mean; if a teacher is actually being mean to students, school principals can work with the teacher to improve the situation

SUSPENSION AND EXPULSION

Suspension is the result of action taken by the school principal. It is a temporary removal of a student from school and school activities for a short period of time, sometimes three to ten days. The decision to suspend a student is not taken lightly by school principals. Certain regulations exist to protect identified students, but generally speaking, a suspension is a mandatory separation of a guilty student from the rest of the school population. Students that violate school rules of a serious nature are subject to one of two severe school punishments depending on the regulations in the school district and state. While suspension is normally short term, expulsion is removal from school for a longer, specific period of time. This removal is often for the remainder of the school year and is the result of school board action. Parents, of course, have the right to appeal such decisions, following ascribed guidelines.

Questions to Consider

For what reason is a student suspended?
Listen/look for: students are often suspended for showing disrespect toward students or staff members, fighting, gross insubordination, vandalism, and other acts covered within school district policy

Who is authorized to suspend a student?
Listen/look for: in some states the principal can suspend a student for a limited period without school board action

How long can a student be suspended?
Listen/look for: many districts authorize principals to suspend a student up to three days without a formal hearing and up to ten days after conducting a formal hearing with the parents

Who watches a child at home while he is suspended?
Listen/look for: if a child is suspended from school because of his actions it is the parents' responsibility to arrange supervision for the child at home

If a child is disabled, can she still be suspended?
Listen/look for: yes, disabled students can be suspended if the behavior is unrelated to her disability

How does a student keep up in his studies while suspended?
Listen/look for: some schools permit a child to make up work missed while on suspension; others may not permit work to be made up

Why can't a child be paddled instead of being suspended?
Listen/look for: corporal punishment has disappeared from many schools; while some districts allow the principal to act in loco parentis, many principals feel that having an adult punish a child by striking him with a piece of wood sends a poor message

Doesn't suspension punish the parents more than the student?
Listen/look for: the intent of a suspension is to help the child realize that there are consequences to misbehavior; any inconvenience to the parents is the fault of the student's action and not the school responding to that action

If parents disagree with the suspension, to whom can they appeal?
Listen/look for: in many school districts a student being considered for a suspension is permitted a hearing involving the parents, student, and principal; if the suspension stands after the hearing, the parents can always appeal to the principal's supervisor or superintendent

What if a parent calls his lawyer?
Listen/look for: in most cases, school principals are authorized to administer school board policy; if the policy states that the consequence for an offence is suspension, the principal is merely doing his job; a call from a lawyer does not alter the obligation of the principal to carry out the approved school board policy

What if a parent has a friend on the school board?
Listen/look for: once again, the principal is normally carrying out the directives of the school board; school board members should be aware of the policies that are being enforced

Doesn't suspension violate a child's right to a free and appropriate education (FAPE)?
Listen/look for: most state school laws permit the temporary removal of students that interfere with the education of others, violate school rules, or pose a threat to others in the school

How many students were suspended from this school last year?
Listen/look for: several states require schools to submit reports on the number of incidents of violence, drug possession, weapon possession, and so on; these reports are usually public record and can be obtained, with adequate notice, from the school district office

How Is a Student Expelled?

Students are expelled from school for violating a school rule or district policy, such as a weapon violation, gross disrespect, threatening others, or other serious infractions. Expulsions are only possible with school board approval. Before the school board votes on a motion to expel, the student is entitled to a due process hearing. In many schools the expulsion process includes the following:

- The principal investigates the allegations.
- The principal informs the parents in writing and requests a conference.
- An informal hearing is held with the parents and student.
- If warranted, the student is suspended pending the board hearing.
- The principal contacts the superintendent and requests an expulsion hearing before the board.
- A formal hearing is held where the student has legal counsel and the district solicitor presents the issues under argument to the school board or a committee of the board.
- The board either expels the student or takes other action at the next school board meeting.
- In most cases the expelled student may return to the home district after the designated expulsion period has elapsed if certain criteria are met. The student must attend classes at another approved school during the expulsion period.

Questions to Consider

What does expulsion mean?
Listen/look for: an action of the school board whereby a student is excluded from attending the home school for an extended period of time

Under what circumstances could a child be expelled?
Listen/look for: excluding a student from school is a serious matter; normally, a student may be expelled for violating rules including drug possession, weapon possession, aggression against a teacher, or terrorist acts

If a child is not formally identified but the parent thinks his child has a disability, can he still be expelled?
Listen/look for: exclusion of special education students is normally regulated by special sections of the state school code relating to rights to education; in cases involving students covered under the Individuals

with Disabilities Education Act (IDEA), the district will fulfill its obligation to educate the child; children "thought to be an exception" may be protected by IDEA

Where does the child go to school if she is expelled from her home school?

Listen/look for: normally parents are responsible for finding an alternative educational institution for their child to attend; in some cases, when the parents cannot find an alternative school, the home school district must make a provision for providing an education for the student

Who expels a student?

Listen/look for: in many states the school board formally expels a student based on a recommendation from the school superintendent

Can the student return to school after the expulsion?

Listen/look for: most expulsions are for a specific period of time; after the term of the expulsion is served the student may return to his home school

How many students were expelled last year from this school?

Listen/look for: school records relating to suspensions and expulsions (not including the student names) are public record and may be reviewed at reasonable times

Can a student make up the work he misses while suspended or expelled?

Listen/look for: normally a student can make up work while suspended, but during expulsion work must be completed at another educational institution

Can a child play sports while suspended?

Listen/look for: in most cases when a student is suspended from school she cannot participate in extracurricular activities including sports; students expelled cannot participate in extracurricular activities at the home school

What Purpose Does Detention Serve?

School detention serves several purposes in most schools. It exerts pressure on students to deter them from further violation of school

rules. It warns other students that the school is serious about enforcement of school rules. It teaches students that there are consequences to
their actions.

Questions to Consider

Why are students assigned detention?
Listen/look for: detention may be assigned for any one of a number of
reasons such as horseplay, inappropriate behavior, insubordination, loi-
tering, inappropriate language, disruption, tardiness, and skipping class

Who assigns after-school detention?
Listen/look for: some schools allow teachers to assign "teacher detention" as part of its adoption of reasonable rules and regulations for disciplining students, while almost all schools permit principals to assign "office detention"; in the case of teacher detention, the teacher assigning the
punishment usually stays with the student. Typically the principal or assistant principal assigns a staff member to supervise office detention

Doesn't keeping a child after school punish the parents?
Listen/look for: the primary purpose of detention is to teach the student
that there are consequences for inappropriate behavior; any inconvenience to parents is the fault of the student that committed the infraction

Can a child serve his detention in the morning before school starts?
Listen/look for: some schools may be able to make provisions for students to attend a detention before school; often it depends on the time
school starts and the availability of supervisory staff

Why can't a child serve detention during the school day?
Listen/look for: serving detention during the school day would mean
that the student is missing a part of the regular school program; detention is meant to be a punishment and not a replacement for a regular
session during the school day

Why can't a parent just punish his child at home in lieu of detention?
Listen/look for: while all schools appreciate the support of parents in
the disciplining of students, it is important that schools administer discipline at school

Who supervises detention?
Listen/look for: certified teachers are normally assigned to supervise detention

Are both students involved in a fight assigned detention?
Listen/look for: fair and consistent administration of school rules usually requires that students determined to be of equal guilt be assigned punishment of equal severity

Aren't Teachers Supposed to Monitor Behavior?

Yes, teachers are the individuals primarily responsible for the enforcement of classroom and school rules. As the person working closest with students, the teacher is in the best position to observe violations and carry out ascribed consequences. Occasionally these consequences include the student being referred to the principal. Teachers are in their positions primarily to provide an education to children. Anything that interferes with the classroom environment affects student learning and must be addressed. Students that violate school rules and interfere with other students' learning are either disciplined by the teachers or the principal.

Questions to Consider

Don't teachers monitor and control student behavior?
Listen/look for: yes, all staff members are to monitor and attempt to control student behavior; during much of the day, teachers are engaged in teaching within the classrooms and routinely impose their own mild forms of discipline

What types of discipline problems do principals handle in a typical day?
Listen/look for: most principals, depending on the grade levels in the school, may in any one day encounter problems related to tardiness, disrespect, fighting, horseplay, arriving late for class, skipping class, locker violations, stealing, fire code violations, swearing, inappropriate gestures, dress code violations, cutting school, hazing, aggression, bomb threats, drug violations, and weapon possession

Can a principal keep two agonistic students apart?

Listen/look for: typically, principals try to keep students apart if there is a valid reason; students assigned to the same classes are difficult to separate; teachers are instructed to move students apart within classes; students may be warned to avoid each other

Isn't it best to let the students work it out themselves?

Listen/look for: in a perfect world allowing students to work out their differences would be wonderful; at times, principals will suggest that students talk out their problems through a peer mediation program; sometimes adult intervention is necessary

Will the school pay the doctor bills when a bully injures a student?

Listen/look for: the school is not responsible for the action of students upon the person of other students; parents seeking injury claims should contact the parents of the offending student; many times a police report must be filed before any legal action can be pursued

Doesn't a child have a right to an education?

Listen/look for: yes, every child has the right to a free and public education

Can parents have a copy of their child's rights?

Listen/look for: most student handbooks include sections that outline student rights (and responsibilities)

How can a principal arbitrarily take rights away?

Listen/look for: schools are not to act in an arbitrary or capricious manner

Can parents appeal to the courts to overrule the principal's decision?

Listen/look for: courts do not wish to become involved in cases related to schools; in many cases they prefer that the aggrieved parent go through the proper procedures, leading to a hearing before the school board

Can a child's special placement be unilaterally changed?

Listen/look for: no, a principal cannot arbitrarily change a child's special placement; individual education plans are a contract between the parents and the school entity; any alterations must be agreed to by both parties unless a due process proceeding takes place

What about Freedom of Speech?

Students do not leave their freedom of speech outside the school-house. But this freedom only applies when it does not interfere with others' freedoms. We all know it is illegal to yell "Fire!" in a crowded theater. Likewise, it is not permissible to show disrespect, harass others, use obscene language, or commit racial slurs in school.

Questions to Consider

Can't a child speak freely without being punished in school?
Listen/look for: in most cases students have the right to express their opinions as long as it does not adversely affect the educational process, interfere with the safety of others, threaten the welfare of the school community, encourage unlawful activity, or interfere with the rights of others

Doesn't a child have a right to her own opinion?
Listen/look for: yes, every child has the right to her opinion if it does not violate the stipulations mentioned earlier

Why can't a child express his concerns in the school paper?
Listen/look for: articles published in a school paper, on school property, funded by school funds may be regulated by school officials; normally criticism of a school or school administrators cannot be censored

When can the school principal censor articles in the student paper?
Listen/look for: as long as the article is not libelous, is not obscene, or does not cause a substantial disruption of the educational process, it is usually not restricted

HOMEWORK

Properly assigned homework reinforces lessons taught in the classroom and provides practice of skills under study. Teachers vary in their application of homework, but most teachers use it in some form. Written assignments, long-term projects, research work, computer reference, and supplemental work may be considered homework. Parents should welcome the chance to observe the work habits of their children while completing homework and use it as an opportunity to become involved in their children's education. Parents should not do homework for their children. Providing assistance and discussing the assignments with children is normally appropriate.

Questions to Consider

What can a parent do if he cannot help his child with her homework?
Listen/look for: at some point, many parents become frustrated because they either do not understand the homework assignment or the material is unfamiliar to them; homework is normally assigned for the student based on work undertaken in class, and as such, it is often a review of skills taught; parents certainly can help students understand concepts contained within homework, but the students should do the work

What can a parent do when she disagrees with the type of homework assigned?
Listen/look for: concerns related to homework should be discussed with the assigning teacher; clarification of expectations should help the parent understand the reason behind assignments; if continued problems are experienced a conference with the principal may be necessary

Does the school board know what homework assignments are given?
Listen/look for: normally the school board does not know the specifics regarding homework assignments; unless a problem arises or parents complain to board members, the routine operation of classes is left to the teachers and principals

What if a child is too busy with soccer, dance, or skating to do homework?
Listen/look for: parents have to make choices: what is more important, a child's education or the soccer game, learning or attending a dance rehearsal; for a student, education is a full-time job; extracurricular activities should not be the primary focus

What if a child refuses to do his homework?
Listen/look for: continued refusal to do homework calls for immediate action on the part of the parent; conferences with the teacher, involvement

of the student support team, or meetings with the principal may provide assistance

How important is homework as a teaching tool?

Listen/look for: homework can be an excellent tool for practice of a newly learned skill; homework should not be busy work; it needs to be an assignment of reasonable length requiring quality effort

What if a child does not understand his homework?

Listen/look for: many hours of frustration occur when a student fails to remember or his notes do not clarify details about the homework assigned; if parents are unable to help the child understand the homework assignment, writing a note to the teacher explaining the situation would help; students need to be reminded how important it is to write down the exact homework assignment

Where can a parent get help if she does not understand the assignment?

Listen/look for: in some schools a website is available to clarify homework assignments; usually it is best to try to do as much of the homework as possible; the parent should write a note to the teacher and remind the child to get the complete assignment the next time

Will the teacher answer questions at home about the assignment?

Listen/look for: most teachers would prefer that parents not call them at home regarding homework assignments; because homework assignments are normally practice of topics and procedures covered in class, unfinished homework assignments are usually not a major problem (unless it is a habit)

What is a reasonable length of time to spend on homework?

Listen/look for: the amount of time allotted for working on homework depends to a large extent on the age of the child; many educators feel that approximately fifteen or thirty minutes of homework for a primary child, thirty to sixty minutes for upper elementary, and sixty minutes to two hours for high school students is typical; students in higher grades usually have more extensive reports, projects, and assignments

What if a teacher assigns too much homework?
Listen/look for: if there is a pattern of extensive assignments that the parent feels is beyond reason, the teacher should be contacted; often what one parent views as excessive another parent sees as appropriate

How Does Cooperative Learning Differ from Copying Each Other's Work?

Cooperative learning, when properly used, permits students to participate in a group work session leading to a conclusion where all involved have played a part. Normally, participants assume various roles within the cooperative group to enable each to contribute to the combined solution. One student may serve as the recorder, one as a leader, one as a timekeeper, and the rest as active participants in the discussion. It is not designed to permit one student to do all of the work while the rest of the group does little.

Cooperative learning is quite different from copying from each other. Students copying from each other rely on one individual to do the work; then they merely copy the finished work, calling it their own. This normally results in little learning on the part of those copying. In cooperative learning, all of the participants share ideas, concepts, and the work experience for the mutual benefit of all.

Questions to Consider

Who assigns the students to the various cooperative groups?
Listen/look for: normally either teachers select and assign roles or students are permitted to select roles within the group

How does the teacher monitor the individual contributions of the students within groups?
Listen/look for: usually, the teacher walks around during the activity, listens, and asks questions regarding the progress of each group and the individual contributions of group members

Aren't cooperative learning groups just an easy lesson for the teacher?
Listen/look for: cooperative learning groups are not easier to work with; specific guidelines need to be conveyed to the students, and the teacher must be alert to assess the work habits of each team

Why is it permissible to work in groups sometimes but not at other times?
Listen/look for: teachers use many approaches in teaching; role playing, small group work, individual assignments, and cooperative learning are often used to meet the needs of the students

STUDENT RESPONSIBILITIES

Students are the reason schools exist. But while they serve as the heart and soul of all schools, they also have responsibilities. Parents should understand the responsibilities of their children in relation to schools and encourage and promote adherence to all school rules and regulations. Review of student handbooks and guidelines serves as a routine reference and should lead to discussions between children and their parents.

Is Attendance Mandatory?

To learn in school, a child must be in school. State law mandates attendance in public school, and educational officials are required to document and submit reports of students enrolled. Not only does attendance affect state reimbursement payments to some schools, it also influences some state test results and school standings.

Schools attempt to help students develop good work habits, including a work ethic of reporting as required. When individual students either refuse or are unable to attend school, legal implications are implemented, and parents may be subject to court-imposed fines.

Questions to Consider

What if a child is consistently out of school because of illness?
Listen/look for: children with repeated health-related absences should be under a doctor's care; nurses in many schools will check to see why a student is missing excessive numbers of school days; in some schools parents are encouraged to arrange for home instruction if the number of days missed is jeopardizing a child's ability to master school subjects

Can a child stay home to take care of an ill sibling?
Listen/look for: in most schools it is illegal for a student to remain at home to take care of a sibling; all states have attendance laws and specific allowable reasons for student absences; these may include personal illness, impassible roads, quarantine, or other reasons listed in state school codes; parents that permit students to violate the state compulsory attendance laws are subject to fines

How can a principal take parents to court if their child refuses to go to school?
Listen/look for: in many states parents are responsible for seeing that their child does not violate the compulsory attendance laws

If a child is eighteen, does he have to go to school?
Listen/look for: in many states students over the age of seventeen may become emancipated and may not be required to attend school

How does a student's attendance affect her grades?
Listen/look for: in most schools poor attendance is not part of the grading system, but students that miss excessive amounts of school days often experience increased failure and poor grades

If a student does well on the tests, why does he have to be in school every day?
Listen/look for: compulsory school attendance laws typically mandate the attendance of children at school while under the age of eighteen

What If a Child Disagrees with the Rules?

Rules are written for the common good. As a result, some individuals may sometimes feel that their freedom is being jeopardized. But most would agree that a society without rules is headed for self-destruction. Schools are small societies and must have rules for efficient operation. Parents should remind students they are to follow rules even if they disagree with them. Certainly, students can work to have rules reconsidered and changed, but until that occurs it is their responsibility, as members of an organization, to adhere to existing rules and regulations.

Questions to Consider

If a child disobeys a poor rule, why is he disciplined?
Listen/look for: once again, a school cannot maintain order if individual students have the option to decide what rules need be followed and what rules can be disregarded

Can a child circulate a petition to change an unreasonable rule?
Listen/look for: in many schools petitions may be circulated if done so in an orderly, nondisruptive manner and with the permission of the principal

If a child does not have enough time to get to class, how can she be considered late?
Listen/look for: schools run on a time schedule; students are normally provided with sufficient time to reach classes; if students are negligent in timely movement they may be subject to consequences; if a general concern is voiced about insufficient time between classes, modification may need to be made

What If the Teacher Does Not Respect a Child?

Any cases of social, racial, or sexual harassment should be brought to the attention of the school principal at once. Every individual has a right to be respected and should, in turn, respect others. Where disrespect or harassment is found to exist, school rules must be enforced to eliminate it. All staff members, teachers, and principals are required to report such negative behavior and carry out disciplinary action where necessary. Staff members, as well as students, that display disrespect toward children are subject to disciplinary action.

Questions to Consider

What happens if the teacher makes fun of a child's name?
Listen/look for: teachers are not permitted to criticize or make fun of students or their family names; bringing the issue to the teacher's attention usually takes care of the matter

What if a teacher calls a student a nickname she dislikes?
Listen/look for: teachers are not permitted to use nicknames or pet names that upset students; bringing the issue to the teacher's attention usually takes care of the matter

What if a teacher picks on a boy because of his race or gender?
Listen/look for: harassment of any kind should not be tolerated on the part of teachers; parents should meet with the teacher or principal at once

Must a Child Always Cooperate with Teachers?

Children should be required to cooperate with all teachers as they endeavor to teach. While individual students may not always want to complete assigned tasks, it is imperative that they put forth effort. Often, students try to avoid things they do not understand or things they are not particularly good at. However, if they never venture into new areas and attempt to experience new challenges, a learning opportunity is lost.

Questions to Consider

What if a teacher contradicts what a parent has told a child?
Listen/look for: normally, teachers are very careful to present information that has been commonly accepted; if a parent discovers that a teacher is providing false or inappropriate information to students, a conference should be scheduled

Must a Child Follow a Rule If It Is Stupid?

Some people may feel that stopping at a traffic light when there is no approaching traffic is stupid. Others may feel signing in at the school office is a waste of time and unnecessary. But, like traffic rules or security regulations, most school rules are based on a perceived need. Yes, a child should follow all rules until they are changed.

Questions to Consider

How can a child be expected to follow a rule he does not understand?
Listen/look for: teachers typically explain all rules to their classes, and student handbooks are distributed to students and parents; if a student does not understand a rule he should inquire and clarify its meaning; unless a student has a disability that would prohibit his understanding, he must be held accountable

If a parent disagrees with a rule, how does she get it changed?
Listen/look for: parents that object to a school rule should contact the school principal; parents that disagree with a school district rule or policy should contact the school superintendent

If a rule is against a parent's religion, how can it be changed?
Listen/look for: parents with a religious objection to a rule should consult the school principal to discuss the matter

If a parent does not believe in a certain holiday celebration, can his child remain at home that school day?
Listen/look for: absence from school must meet state guidelines to comply with compulsory attendance laws; students opposed to holiday celebrations in school may be permitted to read in the library or do other nonsectarian activities in lieu of the celebration

What if a parent's religion does not allow her child to sing holiday music?
Listen/look for: meetings with the school principal and music teacher can usually provide alternative activities for nonparticipants

Why does this school celebrate Christian holidays and not holidays in other religions?
Listen/look for: many schools have included celebrations other than Christian holidays in their school calendars

Can a child leave school to attend a religious service?
Listen/look for: many states allow up to one hour per week for students to attend scheduled religious services

Can a child pray in school?
Listen/look for: individual students are permitted to pray in school; organized group religious services are generally not permitted during the school day

If a child cannot physically adhere to a rule, how can he follow it?
Listen/look for: any inability to follow a rule because of a physical or health-related problem needs to be discussed with the principal

Why does a grade in physical education keep a child off the honor roll?

Listen/look for: honor rolls are created to recognize students that have done exceptionally well in earning school grades; in some schools only academic courses are counted toward membership on an honor roll; in some schools all subjects are counted (some are weighted less than others); discussions with the principal usually clarify the criteria for honor roll membership

What If a Child Does Not Willingly Participate?

Some children are more actively involved in class activities than others. This is a common condition in most schools. Encouragement from parents and teachers can help the student see the value of participation. It has been found, in many cases, that involvement in a wide range of school activities promotes learning. As stated in chapter 1, students get about as much out of school as they put into it.

Questions to Consider

If a child is poor at physical activities, does he have to participate in physical education classes?

Listen/look for: yes, most school plans of study include classes in physical education; students that have difficulty with physical activity need the instruction provided in physical education classes

If a child is shy does, she have to participate in class discussions?

Listen/look for: the best way to overcome shyness is to engage in conversation; discussing the shyness with the teacher may reveal ways to help the child cope with her shyness and improve her communication skills

Is shyness a phase she is going through?

Listen/look for: many students experience some type of shyness; usually involving students in activities related to their strengths (sports, reading, plays) will help develop the self-esteem needed to reduce shyness and the fear of speaking in public

Does class participation affect a child's grades?
Listen/look for: in many classes, participation is an important component; learning to express oneself is a valuable asset both in school and out; depending on the type of class, participation may count toward earned grades

If a child feels embarrassed, does he have to stand and recite?
Listen/look for: unless a speech problem exists, a child needs to develop skills in communication; few youngsters look forward to being called on to recite, but it is part of the learning process; teachers, once aware of the concern, may be able to formulate plans to permit the student to recite easier passages

What If a Child Is Not a Good Listener?

Listening is a skill, and as with all skills, the level of development differs among children. Some children may have a short attention span or be easily distracted. Others may find the classroom is not conducive to learning, or the child may have a hearing problem. Regardless of the reason, it is important that children learn to concentrate on the lesson at hand.

Questions to Consider

What if a child has a short attention span?
Listen/look for: many children at a young age have short attention spans; learning to focus is part of growing up; in severe cases consultation with a doctor may be called for; in most cases techniques are instituted to redirect the student to the task at hand

What if other children distract a child?
Listen/look for: teachers attempt to reduce the distractions within the classroom to a minimum; when and if distractions occur, students may need redirection by the teacher

What if a child is a kinetic learner?
Listen/look for: experienced teachers know that children learn in different ways; many class presentations permit students to learn and work in kinetic, verbal, and visual ways

What if a child has a hearing loss?
Listen/look for: once teachers are informed of the hearing loss, they will take steps to mitigate the situation by moving the child closer to the front of the room; speaking directly toward the child and adapting any class activities to accommodate the child may be helpful

Can the teacher prepare notes for a child?
Listen/look for: note taking is an important skill for all children to learn; if physical limitations prohibit a child from taking his own notes, teachers will normally permit a friend to take notes for them

What If a Child Does Not Complete Work in a Timely Manner?

It is important that children do schoolwork in a quiet, well-lit area away from television and other distractions. Often it is wise for parents to set aside a specific time every day for their child to sit quietly, do their homework, read a book, or work on a project. By developing such a habit, the child begins to realize that he or she will be required to spend quiet time every day regardless of the existence of homework.

Questions to Consider

If a child is a slower worker, how can she finish her classwork on time?
Listen/look for: students work at various speeds; those students that finish classwork earlier are usually provided supplemental work; slower students are encouraged to work as fast as they reasonably can and are generally given adequate time to complete their assignments

If a child has out-of-school activities, how can he complete his homework?
Listen/look for: for children of school age, their priority should normally be their education; sports, dance, skating, and other out-of-school activities, while important, should not interfere with the student's main focus—his schoolwork

What If a Child's Behavior Is Inappropriate?

If every child came to school ready to learn, working at his or her developmental level and behaving appropriately, teaching would be greatly enhanced. The teaching of children requires the teacher to vary classwork, adapt instructional methods, and meet the needs of a variety of students. Behavior problems exist in every classroom, and dealing with and correcting that behavior is one of the teacher's many tasks. Working with the teacher or the student support team, parents can be a great help in teaching children the appropriate behavior for the school setting.

If parents feel that their child is not behaving appropriately for his or her age, consultation with the school guidance counselor or principal is recommended.

Questions to Consider

What if a child is immature?

Listen/look for: normally, immaturity is a matter of acting in a childish manner; most children experience periods of immaturity and then outgrow it; if immature behavior continues, consultation with the teacher, principal, student support team, or physician may be needed

What if a child is seeking attention?

Listen/look for: much of the misbehavior in school is the result of a child seeking attention; attention-seeking behavior can sometimes be dealt with through increased attention being given to positive things a child does; if some students do not receive the attention they crave in a positive way, they may resort to negative behavior

What if a child wants to be thrown out of school?

Listen/look for: occasionally a child may want to be suspended from school; often this occurs because the student desires to be with a parent, is trying to avoid a stressful situation at school, or is experiencing some other traumatic event; the first thing to do in such cases is to find the root of the problem and address that issue

What if a child is worried about her very ill grandmother?
Listen/look for: school officials understand that children react differently to a loved one's illness or death; parents concerned about such matters should contact the teacher, nurse, guidance counselor, or principal to help the child cope with the situation

RETENTION AND ACCELERATION

Questions to Consider

Can a child be retained if the parent does not think he is ready for the next grade?
Listen/look for: retention of a student in a grade is usually not the best approach; while some students in the primary grades may not be developmentally ready for the next grade, many feel it is best to keep the child with his classmates and provide extra help; many educators have found that retaining a student creates discipline problems and reduces feelings of self-worth

If a child is developmentally delayed, should she be retained in kindergarten another year?
Listen/look for: most educators agree that if a child must be retained, kindergarten is the best (and some say the only) time to do so; retaining a child before she establishes a circle of friends and before she actually realizes she is falling behind others is a consideration

If the school wants to retain a child, can his parent appeal the decision?
Listen/look for: normally retaining a child is a joint decision between the parents and the school; many schools have found the mandatory retention of a child, without parental support, results in the loss of parental support and resentment for many years

If a child has mastered the entire current grade level curriculum, can she be moved to another grade level?
Listen/look for: skipping a grade is usually not a good idea; students need to be involved with their appropriate age groups for socialization and maturation reasons; most students that appear to be advanced at

one grade tend to moderate and return more toward the norm in future grades

If a child is not being challenged, can he be moved to a higher grade?
Listen/look for: some children express the feeling that they are bored in school; however, many times their grades do not display a thorough mastery of required skills; discussions with the teacher would be needed to see if the child needs more challenging work, requires placement in a gifted class, or merely complains of being bored because he "thinks" he has mastered the basic requirements

CHAPTER 6

The District

THE SCHOOL BOARD

School boards are either appointed or elected by the registered voters within their communities. Regardless of the method of obtaining their office, once in their position, members have only one vote on issues coming before the board. In some cases it is frustrating to new board members that they cannot change the policy, procedure, or curriculum they previously opposed without the cooperation of a majority of the other board members. There is no doubt that some individuals run for, and may be elected to, the board because of their positions on a single issue. People have been elected to boards to remove a superintendent, to fire a particular teacher or principal, to change a disliked policy, to implement or remove a new course of study, or as an attempt to micromanage the schools. It is only after they are seated on the board that they realize their one vote can change little.

Various special groups may work for the appointment or election of particular individuals to the board. Teacher groups often support candidates sympathetic to their working conditions, concerned citizens sometimes back candidates that pledge not to raise taxes, and religious organizations have sponsored candidates in the hopes of overturning past board decisions counter to their beliefs.

Questions to Consider

What does a school board really do?

Listen/look for: school boards are the ruling bodies of most school districts; they approve all rules and policies, hire and dismiss employees, negotiate contracts, rule on cases of student expulsion, pass school budgets, and monitor school finances

Are board members elected or appointed in this district?

Listen/look for: appointment of school board members is used in some districts; in other districts school board members are elected by public voters

Why do we need school boards?

Listen/look for: many people feel that school boards are needed to monitor the operation of schools as a watchdog for the public; because public tax money is usually the major funding for schools, most communities want a board of school directors to approve and monitor all school budgetary issues

How Does the School Board Communicate with the Public?

School boards do not normally send notices home with children. Routinely, informational items related to school boards are included in notices sent from the individual school principals, articles in the media, or issues discussed at open board meetings. School boards are in existence to operate school districts in a manner that is fiscally and educationally sound. They gather data, form policies, and delegate the implementation of their decisions to superintendents, principals, and teachers. As such, the responsibility to disseminate information to the public is delegated to others within the district.

Questions to Consider

Can a parent see the minutes of school board meetings?

Listen/look for: minutes of school board meetings and subcommittee meetings are public record

Are all school board meetings open to the public?

Listen/look for: school board meetings are open to the public for all official business with certain exceptions, such as executive sessions and personnel matters; negotiations may be held during executive sessions; in some states school boards discussing school business in private violates the Sunshine Laws (Pennsylvania)

Can a parent speak at the school board meeting?

Listen/look for: routinely, members of the community can speak at a school board meeting; some boards require a written request to speak; some boards require prior notice of the desire to speak; some boards permit individuals to speak on a subject without prior notice; in almost all cases boards reserve the right to limit the length of the speech

Is the school board meeting televised?

Listen/look for: in some districts general school board meetings are broadcast on either district-operated or public television channels

Are school board members paid?

Listen/look for: no, school board members are not paid in the vast majority of districts

How long do board members serve?

Listen/look for: in many districts school board members serve between four and six years on the board

Do board members ever listen to parents?

Listen/look for: yes, school board members usually are very concerned about the viewpoints of their constituency; if they are elected members, and wish to be reelected, they often support the feelings expressed by the public

How does a parent contact a school board member?

Listen/look for: all educational central offices have the names of their school board members

What gives the school board the right to raise taxes?

Listen/look for: in most states the board of school directors, or school board, has the legal authority to raise taxes (often through increased mills of taxation) to support schools; in some areas school budgets are placed on referendums

How do board members with only a high school education know how to run schools?
Listen/look for: wise school board members rely on the superintendent of schools to provide information about educational issues; often individual board members have expertise that is helpful in discussions related to school business; many states provide training in procedures related to school board operation, and many districts hold in-services for their own boards on relevant issues

Do board members attempt to micromanage schools?
Listen/look for: they should not micromanage schools; boards hire superintendents and principals for the day-to-day operation of schools; trained educators are the most qualified to run schools, with school board direction

How Is the School Board Actually Involved in Schools?

School boards, as the governing bodies of schools, have an impact on the financial operation of schools, the curriculum used, the quality of teachers hired, and the overall stability of the school district. The board, as a group, is an arm of the state and accountable to the state. Individual board members are answerable to the citizens in the community. While normally elected (some states) or appointed, they sit in a decision-making position and consider the recommendations of district-employed educators, namely the superintendent of schools. As requests are made through the superintendent's office, the board, as a group, listens, discusses, and renders decisions on issues affecting the operation of schools. Hopefully, boards of school directors (or school boards) keep the welfare of students as their primary focus. But, in some cases, individual board members may become blinded by the need to reduce or limit tax increases, and the overall quality of education may suffer. Parents concerned about the possibility of declining quality in their schools need to become vocal at public board meetings. It is only through public reaction to reductions in school programs or unjustified increases in school taxes that boards typically reconsider their actions. While the school board is a watchdog over the educators' use of public money, the public needs to keep a watchful eye on the actions of the school board.

Questions to Consider

Does the school board interview and hire teachers?
Listen/look for: in some districts they do; in many districts, boards delegate that responsibility to the superintendent, who in turns delegates the responsibility to principals; the school board then considers the recommendations

Does the school board approve all rules?
Listen/look for: all school district policies are approved by the board; individual school rules and classroom rules are not normally approved directly by the board, but all school and classroom rules are to be consistent with approved board policy

How does the school board know if a student should be expelled?
Listen/look for: boards listen carefully to the testimonies of students, parents, teachers, and principals to determine the innocence or guilt of accused students

Who runs the district, the superintendent or the school board?
Listen/look for: in most districts the school board is responsible for running the district; superintendents are hired to oversee and manage the educational program of the district; a wise school board will involve the superintendent in all aspects of the district, from finance to transportation, because all activities of a school district relate to the education of children

To whom does the school board answer?
Listen/look for: in many states school board members, as public servants, ultimately answer to the public; in districts where the school board is elected, the voters have the opportunity to voice their support or opposition to actions of a board member at the polls

What if a parent disapproves of some action of the school board?
Listen/look for: as public servants, board members are obliged to listen to the concerns of all community members; speaking at board meetings,

letters to individual board members, or public support for opposing viewpoints are freedoms we all have

What does the school board know about running an educational program?

Listen/look for: after study, training, and experience on the board, members should grow in their insight, knowledge, and ability to operate a school district; in many districts the terms of school board members are staggered so that only a part of the board is up for reelection at a time

SCHOOL DISTRICT POLICIES

Every organization needs guidelines and rules for proper operation. Schools are no different. School policies are the guidelines and regulations considered, discussed, and approved by the school board to be implemented in the schools by administrators. Generally, policies are the result of some perceived need within the school community. Most schools have seen a need to develop policies regarding drug use, student discipline, student dress codes, harassment of students, emergency procedures, attendance, and students driving to school, to list only a few. Policy books often contain a multitude of policies necessary to regulate school districts composed of hundreds or thousands of students and employees.

While parents can certainly have input into the formation of policies through their elected school board members, usually a committee of educators, guided by the district solicitor, develops recommended policies. After the school board discusses and approves these new policies, they are printed, distributed, implemented, and enforced by school principals.

Questions to Consider

Isn't the use of common sense enough without all of the policies?

Listen/look for: common sense is often a major part of school policy, but a high degree of common sense may be lacking in some individuals; it is necessary to have common rules, regulations, and policies to ensure consistency in application and fairness in administration

What if a parent disagrees with a policy?
Listen/look for: policies are to be followed until they are rewritten or canceled; individuals that disagree with current policy have every right to discuss that opposition with teachers, principals, and board members in an effort to have the policy changed

What if a child is falsely accused and the policy is unfair?
Listen/look for: typically it is not the policy that may be unfair but the interpretation or enforcement of the policy; in cases where a child is falsely accused and thought to be guilty of violating a school district policy, the interpretation of the policy needs to be examined

Who writes school policies?
Listen/look for: often school administrators in consultation with district solicitors develop policies; school boards then discuss the proposed policies and either review, approve, or dismiss them

Can a parent write a policy and have it approved?
Listen/look for: contributions from parents are welcome at all times; school officials are usually open to ideas and suggestions from parents

How do parents find out what policies exist?
Listen/look for: parents should refer to student handbooks for brief descriptions of policies and consult the district's policy book for complete information related to a specific policy

Do all principals and teachers follow policies?
Listen/look for: school district policies are to be carried out as approved by the board; school principals are responsible for carrying out the directives of the school board and superintendent; teachers are responsible for carrying out the directives of the principals

Are policies ever changed or updated?
Listen/look for: yes, school policies should be reviewed and updated periodically; as society changes, school rules must change as well

Why are parents not given a copy of the district policies?
Listen/look for: in most districts the number of policies is very large, and providing every parent with a copy would be a tremendous waste of tax money; most parents would have no use for a copy of all school policies

Are all individual school rules approved by the school board?
Listen/look for: no, but all school rules should reinforce and complement school district policies

THE BUDGET

Development of a school budget is a major undertaking for any school
district. The resulting document, often consisting of fifty or more
pages, is open to public examination. Many districts attempt to involve
the public from the early stages in the budgetary preparation. Through
financial committee meetings and general school board meetings, concerned community members have the opportunity to express their opinions related to anticipated revenues and expenditures. In most districts
today, the majority of the school district budget consists of fixed costs
including salaries, benefits, utilities, and loan commitments. Often as
little as 8 or 10 percent of the entire budget is available for nonfixed
cost adjustment. This leaves little room for massive alterations in expenditures (see the section on taxes).

Questions to Consider

How much is the school budget?
Listen/look for: school budgets can range from a few million to several hundred million dollars; the total amount of a school budget
is public record and can be obtained at the central administration
office; individual school budgets also are public record, and information relative to the budgets can be obtained at the individual
schools

How much does it cost to educate a child in this school?
Listen/look for: many elements are included in arriving at a true cost
per pupil; in addition to the costs of instruction (teachers and supplies)
are the costs of transportation (bus maintenance, gasoline, drivers'
wages), utilities in the building (heat, water, sewer, air conditioning),
maintenance (replacement and repair of equipment), and other somewhat hidden costs

Who decides how the money is spent in this district?
Listen/look for: in many states it is ultimately the school board that passes a budget for the school district and decides how tax money will be utilized; in some states the proposed budget is passed or rejected by voters as part of a referendum

Do teachers have all the money they need?
Listen/look for: teachers normally have adequate funds to operate their programs; there are always things that could be bought in addition to needed items; it is the school board's responsibility to support the educational program by providing funding for required courses of study

Can a parent see where the money is spent in this district?
Listen/look for: yes, the entire school budget and how it is to be disbursed are public record; normally monthly statements of current encumbrances, outstanding purchase orders, and balances in accounts are supplied to the school board

TAXES

Financial support of public schools is becoming more difficult every year. As state budgets become tighter, some states have stabilized or reduced state support of schools and, in some cases, postponed payment of funding to districts. The question of property taxes as a foundation for public school financial support has been questioned for years. In response, some states have tried lotteries, taxes of various types, business partnerships, and various funding formulas with mixed success. Regardless of the approach used, no one doubts that education is a big business with nearly one out of four individuals engaged in some aspect of the education system.

Most people would agree that schools need some type of financial support. In fact, recent Gallup polls have indicated that school funding is one of the major concerns of Americans. Many would further agree that some financial assistance is required from the state and federal government. The amount, process of collection, and percent of local effort required for adequate financing of schools are up for debate. As local school expenses continue to escalate because of increases in utilities, wages, fringe benefits, transportation costs, and supplies and equipment additional money is needed. At the same time, interest groups including concerned citizen groups, religious groups, and concerned taxpayer groups often campaign to hold the line on taxes. The move to avoid additional taxes at the local level is not new. But the present situation facing schools including declining standardized test scores, increased operating costs, larger percentages of nonparent taxpayers, and inadequate state support creates a situation where great effort is required to avoid reductions in academic programs.

Questions to Consider

Aren't teachers paid too much for an easy job?

Listen/look for: salaries and fringe benefits are a major part of any school budget; however, when one considers the amount of education required, the additional compulsory course work, the responsibility of the position, and the time on task each day with a room full of children, the hourly wage is not commensurate with most other professions

Why do taxes go up year after year?

Listen/look for: often taxes reflect needed funding for increased utilities, transportation costs, salaries, insurance costs, textbooks and supplies, and other fixed costs; even with increases at the state level of educational funding, often inflation, increased costs of utilities and insurance, and mandates result in reduced revenue at the local level; the public sector (schools) must obtain its funding from the private sector (community) through taxation

Why can't they cut the fat?

Listen/look for: it depends on what is considered "fat"; many districts have reduced supervisory personnel, increased class sizes, maintained old buildings, and reduced the amount of teaching supplies in an attempt to keep taxes down

Parents live within their means without an increase. Why can't schools?

Listen/look for: schools attempt to do so, but just as your fixed costs go up each year, so do the schools'; many schools seek other forms of revenue to reduce reliance on taxes

Some community members have no children. Why do they pay school taxes?

Listen/look for: education benefits the entire community not just the students in the schools; a better educated workforce, higher income levels, a better economy, advanced use of technology, better decisions, and more cultural areas can be the result of a good educational system

Isn't there a lot of waste in schools?

Listen/look for: most schools conduct inventories to assess the need for new supplies; waste is kept to a minimum as much as possible

Isn't a central office a waste of educational money?

Listen/look for: in a well-organized and coordinated school district a central office is critical; volume buying, financial accountability, supervision and coordination of curriculum areas, special education issues, and response to state and federal mandates require an efficient central office

Why do test results decline and taxes go up?

Listen/look for: test results often mirror the number of students taking the test; while the standardized test results in some schools have leveled off or declined in some areas, it does not mean that the quality of education has been reduced

If a child needs special help, is tutoring free?

Listen/look for: tutoring outside of school is typically the responsibility of the parents; schools may supply names of tutors for parent consideration; special help may be available through student support efforts

Does the district get money from the state?

Listen/look for: yes, in all states some money is obtained through state funding, state grants, and subsidy payments; each school receives differing amounts depending on the district's wealth, scarcity and density factors, and other factors that adjust the state contribution

Do school officials try to get money through grants?

Listen/look for: most school districts attempt to increase revenue by applying for grants; some districts have full-time grant writers for the purpose of finding and applying for grants

SPECIAL HELP

Not all children progress through their school careers with ease. It is normal for some children to experience difficulty with one or more subject areas or with the learning process itself. When a child experiences a problem with his or her schoolwork, the parents and teacher involved should meet to assess the problem and plan strategies to help the child achieve more success.

In many schools, special teams of professional educators meet on a regular basis to monitor children that may be experiencing difficulty. These teams, sometimes called student support teams, have the best interests of each child at heart and attempt to remediate the situation. A student support team may be composed of various professionals including the school principal, guidance teacher, classroom teachers, psychologist, or other staff members. Often parents are involved in the process because the support and encouragement of the adults at home is vital to a child's success. Parents should accept this assistance from the school as a very powerful, beneficial aid because professional educators typically have a vast amount of knowledge related to how children learn. They know what strategies might be appropriate, how to help the child structure his or her time, approaches to improve listening skills, methods to assist in social relationships, and steps to take to improve student behavior. Parents bring to the table a keen knowledge of their child's personality, past history, and out-of-school influences (stress factors) that might be affecting school performance.

Whether it is peer pressure, the death of a loved one, poor self-esteem, a learning disability, emotional stress, poor attitude toward school, or a perceived personality conflict with the teacher, the parent and student support team can often help the child adjust.

Questions to Consider

What can a parent do to help his child in school?
Listen/look for: provide a healthy breakfast; read to your child; send your child to school ready to learn; demonstrate support for school

rules; encourage your child to do her very best; stress the importance of a good education

Won't the involvement of the school psychologist automatically result in a special placement?

Listen/look for: no; school psychologists often interview and test children for various reasons; if a child is having difficulties in school, the testing the psychologist administers may help provide answers

Will a child be labeled if the support team helps him?

Listen/look for: student support teams help children in many ways; normally no special placement is required; they help discover ways of adapting the curriculum to meet a child's needs, without a label being placed on the child

What will the meeting with the support team be like?

Listen/look for: often the support team will meet with the parents and discuss strengths, weaknesses, and any factors that may be interfering with a child's learning; parent input is vital to the development of strategies and goals to help the child

Will parents be made to feel it is their fault that their child is not learning?

Listen/look for: no; children have difficulty learning for many reasons; the purpose of the meeting is to help the child, not to point fingers

Identified children receive help. Why can't all students?

Listen/look for: student support teams attempt to help any child that is at risk; identified children have a legal contract with the district (IEP)

What is covered in a gifted program?

Listen/look for: many gifted programs provide students with exercises in logical thinking and creative problem solving, along with other opportunities to challenge their minds

What are the criteria for placement in gifted programs?

Listen/look for: states have different criteria for placement in gifted programs; in some states an IQ of around 130 is required, with a display of gifted behavior in regular classes

Help with Special Problems

From time to time, families experience problems and situations that affect not only the child's home life but school life as well. When such occasions occur, parents need to notify the school and inquire if help can be obtained. The death of a loved one, a divorce, moving to a new neighborhood, custody concerns, legal problems faced by the family, or other life stressors can often be addressed by the school staff in a helpful, educational manner.

Questions to Consider

Can the school help a child while his parents are getting a divorce?
Listen/look for: guidance counselors will often work with students to help them develop coping strategies to deal with their parents' divorce; parents should meet with the counselor to discuss the best approach

Can a parent stop her spouse from seeing her child at school?
Listen/look for: schools must honor the requests of both parents unless there is a court order to the contrary; parental separations have no effect on a parent's rights unless a legal document is on file in the school office

Can the school help a child understand his grandmother's death?
Listen/look for: guidance counselors are trained to deal with children experiencing the loss or possible loss of a loved one; parents should meet with the counselor to discuss the best approach

What if a student is sad and suicidal as the result of her loved one's death?
Listen/look for: parents should meet immediately with the school principal and guidance counselor or psychologist; parents should discuss concerns openly and request a list of available community resources

How can a tutor be obtained?
Listen/look for: some schools will provide parents with a list of approved tutors

Does the school provide and pay for a tutor?
Listen/look for: some schools will attempt to find tutors for students within the faculty; in the majority of cases it is the parents' responsibility to pay for tutoring

What will a tutor cost?
Listen/look for: usually the cost of tutoring is negotiated between the tutor and the parent

When and where will the tutor work with a child?
Listen/look for: tutors sometimes stay after school and work with a child; more often tutors come to the student's home in the evening

Can a child do extra work to better his grade?
Listen/look for: usually extra work will have some influence on a grade, but the major elements of a grade remain the completion of required classwork

What if a child has difficulty with math?
Listen/look for: it is important that parents meet with the math teacher as soon as possible to determine what can be done at home to strengthen her math performance; parents should monitor work carefully and set aside a specific time each night for the child to work on her math assignments

If a parent did poorly in math, won't his son be a poor math student also?
Listen/look for: ability to do math is not inherited; a parent's encouragement can be a great help

What if a student just can't get it?
Listen/look for: every student can learn; alternative methods may be needed and modification of the approaches used may be necessary

Can a parent help a student study over the summer?
Listen/look for: yes, in many cases the school will provide resources to help a child over the summer; summer school may be an option

CHAPTER 7

Support Services

SPECIAL EDUCATION

Identification and placement in special education is occasionally needed to meet the learning needs of some children. Although parents should regard this special placement as a positive opportunity to help their child, some regard this identification as a negative label placed on their child. Unfortunately, in most cases intensive help, alternative testing procedures, and adapted teaching strategies are only possible in specially designed classes. Without the special placement, many children will continue to struggle in school, encountering daily frustration because of a learning disability, social or emotional problem, or other concern that might have been addressed through special education.

Questions to Consider

What if a parent thinks his child has a learning problem?
Listen/look for: concerned parents should meet with the school principal and ask for a screening by the student support team

How does a parent know if her child has a learning disability?
Listen/look for: a screening and evaluation by the school psychologist can reveal a learning disability

Why do some children have learning problems?
Listen/look for: the causes of learning problems are not clear; parents should not feel guilty because their child has a learning problem

How are special classes different from regular classes?
Listen/look for: some special education classes are held within the special educator's classroom; some are conducted as part of the regular teacher's class (regular education initiative, or REI); and some are pullout programs where the special needs child is taught in the special education classroom only for the classes in which he is exhibiting difficulties

If a child is having a problem only in reading, can she go to regular math and science classes?
Listen/look for: normally yes; in many schools special education is provided only in the areas where learning difficulty is present

How can a parent get his child out of special education?
Listen/look for: if his child has been identified as a special needs student (requires parent permission), a parent may elect to institute a due process proceeding; the school will review the status of the student and meet with the parent to discuss proper placement; in cases where the school and parent disagree on the placement of the child, a due process hearing may be scheduled

How can a parent get her child into the gifted program?
Listen/look for: in schools that operate a gifted program, certain criteria are in place to identify students displaying gifted or talented tendencies; parents can often request testing of their child to determine her eligibility

How does a child compare academically with his peers?
Listen/look for: every student's academic record is confidential, but standardized test scores can give parents an indication of the ranking of their child in comparison with his class, school, and state; in some cases national rankings are available

Why can't a child be accelerated?
Listen/look for: most schools do not accelerate children, preferring instead to enrich the child's educational experience; many gifted classes provide opportunities to challenge identified children and enhance their creative and logical thinking abilities

Who writes an individual education plan (IEP)?
Listen/look for: the writing of an IEP is a joint effort of the teacher, the principal, and the parents

What will the IEP say?
Listen/look for: the IEP will outline the program of study and the specific goals for the individual student for the year; in some cases a behavioral plan is included

Will parents have input into their child's educational plan?
Listen/look for: absolutely; parent input is a necessary element

What if a parent wants to discuss the IEP later in the school year?
Listen/look for: IEPs can be reopened at any time; parents need only notify the school of their desire to open the IEP and make adjustments

Will the special placement remain in a child's record?
Listen/look for: a child remains in a special placement until a multidisciplinary team, following due process procedures, alters the placement; the record of a child's placement often remains in the student's permanent file until graduation, after which only specific information related to grades and attendance is maintained

How long will a child remain in special education?
Listen/look for: most students, once identified, remain in special placement throughout the remainder of their schooling; often a learning disability or other reason for special placement is not eliminated, although coping skills are developed by the child

Can special education classes make a child normal?
Listen/look for: every child has some strengths and some areas of weakness; while disabilities seldom completely disappear, special education students can often overcome or learn to cope with their disabilities and lead a successful, meaningful life

TECHNOLOGY

Children are continually surrounded by technology. MTV, music videos, boom boxes, VH1, and other mass media productions are great influences on young people. As a result many schools have incorporated increased use of technology in their classes as a means of maintaining student interest and providing educational opportunity. Even more important, modern businesses require a workforce that is knowledgeable about computers and other technological tools. Schools attempt to meet this need through the use of computers at various grade levels, some as early as kindergarten.

No longer considered a separate subject, computers are often part of regular classroom instruction. Use of word processing programs for English, Spanish, science, social studies, math, and other subjects is becoming more common every year. Today, the use of technology in schools is not a subject of debate; it is a necessity for progressive educational institutions preparing students for the world of tomorrow.

Questions to Consider

Do all schools have computer labs?
Listen/look for: no, some schools choose to place computers in classrooms

Isn't it silly to have a computer for every child?
Listen/look for: it depends on how the computers are being used; in some schools the reliance on computers is very slight, and a lab or bank of computers is sufficient

How are computers used?
Listen/look for: computers are used in various ways; computer classes are conducted; language arts, creative writing, social studies, art, music, and almost any other class can utilize technology if the teacher feels it is appropriate

Isn't a child becoming just a number thanks to computers?
Listen/look for: in most schools students are not mere numbers; they are young, creative, exciting learners in need of a learning experience; few teachers or principals consider students numbers

At what grade level does computer instruction begin?
Listen/look for: some schools have computers available in kindergarten; other schools wait until the child is in primary or intermediate grades

Should a parent buy a computer for his home?
Listen/look for: as students become more and more accustomed to technology it is helpful if they can practice their learned skills at home

Aren't computers just used for games at the elementary level?
Listen/look for: in many schools games are not permitted on school computers; computers are used as important teaching and learning tools

Are computers reducing the quality of handwriting skills?
Listen/look for: hopefully not; students still have to take notes in class, respond to test questions, and complete homework with written work; a balance is needed between use of technology and handwriting

What kinds of computers are used in the school?
Listen/look for: some schools use Macintosh, some IBM, others Gateway; in fact, almost every type of computer is used in some school; parents can consult the school to find out what they are using; it is very helpful if a home computer is similar to those at school because software varies greatly with Windows, Microsoft Word, Excel, and others in common use

How Is Technology Used in the Classroom?

In today's world technological knowledge is a must for success in life. Students at all levels need to work with computers appropriate to their degree of development. At the elementary level children need to become accustomed to the keyboard, various programs available in word processing, and basic maneuvering techniques. As children proceed into higher grades they should be exposed to increased diversity in programs. If one considers the increased use of computers in the work world within the last ten to fifteen years, one can only guess at the heightened degree of need for technological skills that may be needed in the next ten to twenty years.

Other communication tools such as video recording and teleconferencing are now a part of many school systems. As the need to communicate with others, sometimes thousands of miles away, increases, new and enhanced means of reaching out to talk and discuss issues are needed. Exposure to all of the latest advances in communication is vital to a child's education and critical to his or her future.

Questions to Consider

Do teachers use copyrighted material in classes?
Listen/look for: teachers are not permitted to violate the copyright of any written publication; under some circumstances, one copy of copyrighted material may be made for classroom use

How does the principal know if copyrighted material is being used?
Listen/look for: many principals monitor use of photocopiers or spot-check duplications used by teachers

How much photocopied work is used in classes?
Listen/look for: teachers often use many sheets of paper within their classes; photocopying tests, handouts, notices to go home, homework assignments, and worksheets is common

Are all children videotaped in the classroom?
Listen/look for: normally parent permission is required before a student can be videotaped; often parents are notified within the student handbook that if they do not wish to have their child taped, they must notify the school in writing; in some schools videotaping of students for use solely within classes is permitted

What if a parent does not want his child to be videotaped?
Listen/look for: parents that make the school aware that they are opposed to their child being videotaped will have that request honored

Is a child permitted to use a calculator in math class?
Listen/look for: most math teachers want their students to learn and practice math skills without the use of calculators; once the math concepts are mastered, some teachers allow students to use calculators to simplify basic computation as part of story problems

Whatever happened to pencils and paper in the classroom?
Listen/look for: pencils and paper are still used as a valuable tool in most classes

Are computers used in all classes?
Listen/look for: many, indeed most, schools have incorporated computers into the school curriculum; some classes are more prone to use computers: creative writing, science, computer labs, English, and so on

FOOD SERVICE

Providing lunch to children while in school is a means to sustain them for the effort required during their day of schoolwork. While a variety of school lunch programs exist, a great deal of planning is needed to provide children with nutritious food. Sometimes it is difficult to serve children healthy food choices while offering the type of meals that children might like. Some schools are intent on providing a balanced food program that meets the guidelines of state-recommended lunch programs.

In many cafeterias educational assistants, or aides, are responsible for monitoring the behavior of students while eating. In other schools, teachers are assigned the duty of cafeteria supervision. Regardless of the person in the role, students should follow the school rules regarding the cafeteria. Lunch is a time for eating, chatting, and limited socialization, not loud, unruly behavior.

Questions to Consider

What if the cafeteria food is cold and tastes spoiled?
Listen/look for: concerns related to the quality of school lunches should be discussed with the principal; students that find their lunch spoiled or tasting strange should ask to talk to the cafeteria monitor or principal

What if a child is still hungry after eating lunch?
Listen/look for: most schools provide school lunches to sustain students for the duration of the school day; school lunches are not primarily intended to fill students; usually students that have had a healthy breakfast will find school lunches sufficient

What if a child does not like the food served?
Listen/look for: in most schools students have the choice of buying lunch or carrying a lunch from home; in many schools a la carte lunches are provided, or alternative choices are available to students

What if a child gets smaller portions than other students?
Listen/look for: usually portions are measured for individual lunch servings

Why can't a child eat at another table with his friends?

Listen/look for: schools assign student lunch tables for various reasons; some schools want to seat students by homerooms; some may seat students in order of arrival; many schools may separate students because of behavioral issues; some allow students to be seated randomly; most schools will explain their rationale for lunch seating to interested parents

What if a child leaves her table a mess every day?

Listen/look for: students are expected to clean their eating areas before leaving the lunchroom; monitors will usually enforce rules related to proper disposal of food waste and table cleanliness

What if the cafeteria monitor is mean to the children?

Listen/look for: cafeteria monitors are concerned with an orderly lunch procedure; they are there to enforce rules such as remaining seated, keeping food off the floor, quiet talking, and proper cleanup procedures; some students view the enforcement of rules as being mean; if a particular monitor is guilty of "picking on a student," the principal may be contacted

Can a child leave the school during lunchtime?

Listen/look for: some schools (usually high schools) allow an open campus during lunchtime; depending on the school rules, students may be able to walk to nearby convenience stores to purchase lunch; at the elementary level students are typically assigned to eat in the school cafeteria

Can a child have a pizza delivered to school for lunch?

Listen/look for: the delivery of pizza or other out-of-school purchases is usually not permitted; lunch is scheduled for a particular time each day, and deliveries do not always arrive precisely at the time requested; schools attempt to reduce the number of nonessential visitors to the school, and deliveries during the school day make that job much more difficult

Can a child receive a free or reduced lunch?

Listen/look for: every state has criteria established (usually income levels in relation to family size) to meet federal guidelines for free or reduced lunch and breakfast programs; applications may be obtained either at the district office or at the school for parents interested in applying

What if the cafeteria monitor assigns a silent lunch when some of the children are innocent?

Listen/look for: the assignment of a silent lunch to all of the students in a particular lunch period is problematic; while numerous students may be misbehaving there are always students that are completely innocent; it is best to identify those students that are misbehaving and administer appropriate punishment

Can the cafeteria monitor walk around with a cup of coffee during her duties?

Listen/look for: the primary duty of a cafeteria monitor is the supervision of children; anything that interferes with that responsibility should not be permitted

THE SCHOOL BUS

The school bus exists to safely transport children to and from school. That is the sole purpose of the transportation system in a school district. However, at times, behavior of children on the bus or the actions of the bus driver may bring the travel to and from school to the attention of the principal. School districts are very concerned about the behavior of students on buses because it may interfere with the safety of others. Concerns are also raised if the actions of the driver place the safety of the students at risk or could pose other types of danger.

As the individuals responsible for the safety of fifty to seventy students, bus drivers often initiate rules on their buses. Assigning seats to students, making attempts to reduce noise, and insisting that students face forward and remain seated are examples of rules sometimes imposed.

Questions to Consider

What behavior is expected on a school bus?

Listen/look for: reasonably quiet talking and appropriate behavior that does not interfere with the safe transportation of students

Can a bus driver discipline a child?

Listen/look for: normally yes; reassignment of seating and reporting the student to the principal are standard responses to misbehavior; depending on the district transportation rules, a student, after a hearing before the principal, may be removed from the bus for disruptive behavior

Are bus drivers trained in first aid?

Listen/look for: drivers are usually trained to respond to emergencies and render basic first aid

Do bus drivers have to have clearances to drive a bus?

Listen/look for: yes; all school employees must have clearances to work near children

What special training do bus drivers receive to drive a bus?

Listen/look for: in most states school bus drivers must pass a special driving test and are regularly tested on their driving skills

Can a driver make a child get off the bus at a point other than his bus stop?

Listen/look for: usually no; a bus driver is normally permitted to transport a student to and from his bus stop only; in cases of extreme disruption, some districts authorize drivers to take children to the nearest police station or return them to their school; stopping at a babysitter's, a Boy Scout meeting, and so on are not allowed

Does the driver pick the drop-off points for children?

Listen/look for: commonly, bus pick-up and drop-off points are designated by the supervisor of transportation and approved by the school board; distance between stops, distance from school, safety of the stop, adequate room for the bus to stop safely, and other traffic-related issues are considered

Who is responsible for discipline on the buses?

Listen/look for: primarily the bus driver, as the district's representative, is responsible; ultimately, the principal is responsible for administering any consequences as a result of bus behavior

Does the principal always back up the driver in discipline cases?

Listen/look for: principals often support the bus driver in cases of observed misbehavior on the bus; unless a principal has reason to believe that a driver has alternative motives, the employee of the district is assumed to be telling the truth

Can a parent have a driver changed if he is mean?
Listen/look for: normally no, unless verifiable misconduct is proven; a meeting with the driver should be held to discuss the issue

What if a parent hears the bus is out of control?
Listen/look for: concerned parents should report any control issues to the building principal

Can the bus route be changed?
Listen/look for: bus routes are carefully planned to account for the number of children, travel time, and appropriate use of buses and drivers; to change a bus route is a very complex matter

Will the driver let a child off the bus in front of her house?
Listen/look for: once bus routes are established they normally remain the entire year; in some cases buses do pick children up in front of their homes; in other cases, groups of children meet at a central point and are picked up; in cases of temporary disability (e.g., a broken leg) drivers may be able to adjust the pick-up and drop-off points nearer to the student's home

Will the driver wait for a child to come to the bus?
Listen/look for: bus drivers will normally wait a very short period of time for students to come to the bus stop; unless a driver sees a student moving toward his bus in a prompt manner, he may drive away

Why can't the driver honk the horn when she stops in front of a child's house?
Listen/look for: if drivers stopped and honked their horns for every student to exit his home and walk to the bus, it would increase the bus travel time to the school by many, many minutes; it is the student's responsibility to watch for and promptly report to the pick-up area

Why are cameras on some buses?
Listen/look for: cameras have been installed on many school buses for safety reasons; students often deny misbehavior, and videos can usually clarify the behavior; additionally, vandalism and destructive behavior can be documented

Does a child have to have an assigned seat?
Listen/look for: most bus drivers assign seats to student riders; assigning seats to separate disruptive students and for ease in disembarking has proven beneficial

TEMPORARY MEDICAL CONDITIONS

At times, individual students may encounter temporary medical conditions that warrant special considerations at school. Broken legs or arms or temporary hearing or sight loss might be reasons to consider a change in the normal school routine for the child. It is reasonable for parents to expect the school to make accommodations to help their child participate to the fullest extent possible. In any cases of temporary disability, parents need to meet with the principal or student support team to develop plans to meet their child's short-term condition. In some states such a plan is called a 504 plan. This plan is a temporary placement and adaptation of regular studies to meet a temporary need of the child. Parents should inquire at the school regarding the existence of similar placements.

Questions to Consider

What if a child has a temporary injury such as a broken leg?
Listen/look for: most schools will make accommodations to alleviate the stress and hardship of a temporary disability

Can someone carry a student's books?
Listen/look for: normally, yes

Can a student have extra time between classes?
Listen/look for: often, yes

How does a temporarily disabled student get to school?
Listen/look for: if he cannot ride his regular school bus, some districts have lift vans available; parents should discuss the issues with the school principal

Can the student be moved closer to the front of the class?
Listen/look for: if her disability necessitates movement closer to the front of the room it can usually be accommodated

Can the school provide a wheelchair for the student's use in school?
Listen/look for: the availability of a wheelchair depends on the school; some schools have wheelchairs on site, and some do not

Can an aide help the student off the school bus at school?
Listen/look for: usually an educational assistant can assist where needed

What is a chapter 504 plan?
Listen/look for: a chapter 504 allows for adaptations to a course of study because of a temporary disability; a student service plan is developed that modifies the student's schedule, course work, or other areas related to his schooling

Is a 504 plan special education?
Listen/look for: no, a 504 plan is only a temporary plan to meet immediate needs of a student

Will a child be labeled with a 504 plan?
Listen/look for: no, a child is not labeled because of a 504 plan

Is it the same as an IEP?
Listen/look for: no; an IEP is a plan developed for a specific student identified as learning disabled, socially or emotionally disturbed, autistic, or another designation

IN LOCO PARENTIS

Historically, schools have been cast into the role of serving as the parent, or "in loco parentis," for children while they are in school. This section of some school codes grants the same authority to principals and teachers as to parents or guardians regarding the conduct and behavior of students while attending school.

Questions to Consider

What is in loco parentis?
Listen/look for: in some states teachers and principals are granted in loco parentis when supervising students at school; in practical terms it

means that the teacher or principal has the authority to act as the parent in an emergency situation when the parent cannot be reached

Does it mean that teachers can paddle a child?
Listen/look for: no, it does not give school officials permission to use corporal punishment

Does it mean that teachers can grab a child?
Listen/look for: no, it does not give teachers or principals permission to grab or strike a child unless it is in self-defense or to protect another student

Why is it necessary?
Listen/look for: in cases where a child's welfare is at stake and the parent cannot be contacted it is necessary to have an adult authorized to take the needed action

Glossary

The education profession, like many professions, has a unique vocabulary including terms and acronyms that may be unfamiliar to some parents. This can lead to misunderstandings and reduced communication between parents and school officials. Clarifications and explanations of some terms and acronyms found in this book are presented in this glossary. Additional definitions are provided for parent reference. While the definitions provided are commonly accepted, some schools and districts may have unique interpretations somewhat different from those provided here. The following should only be used as a guide when communicating with school principals and teachers.

acceleration. the enhancement of a curricular area to enable a student to work beyond the current level of his peers

ADD/ADHD. attention deficit disorder or attention-deficit/hyperactivity disorder

AWA. administration by walking around

bomb threat. a threat against a school regarding a possible explosive device; usually related to a verbal or written threat indicating the possible existence of a bomb within or near the school site

brainstorming. a technique whereby all participants within a group are invited to suggest ideas related to a topic, and all ideas are accepted without comment

bullying. threats made by one individual toward another individual; threats to harm or injure another person with or without a weapon are a major concern for school administrators

career ladder. a process whereby teachers can progress financially higher on the salary schedule through meeting established criteria

central education office. the district-level administrative offices, normally where the superintendent and other supervisors or directors are housed

certification. a state license to teach, issued by the state to individuals that have met the requirements to teach in the public schools

charter school. a type of privately operated public school; often independently operated within the existing school district

class size. the number of students assigned to a classroom or teacher

clearances. checks to see if employees or potential employees have any criminal history (Act 34) or any record of child molestation (Act 32)

climate/environment/ethos. the surroundings within a building including the relationships among the staff, students, and parents; normally a positive school climate is a goal of administrators because it enhances the learning atmosphere for the children

Columbine-type event. any incident similar to the tragic school shooting at Columbine High School in Colorado, a landmark incident in school violence

cooperative learning. an approach to learning where participants assume various roles while cooperatively working on an assignment

corporal punishment. paddling with the hand or some other object; most schools have discontinued the practice, deciding instead to institute other means of discipline

crisis response team. a group of individuals trained to assist the principal in the event of a dangerous situation in the school; this team, trained in current practices related to crisis management, meets when a risk is evident that could affect the school population

critical incident. an event of an extremely dangerous nature that could possibly endanger the school population and requires immediate action by the principal and crisis response team

cruelty. intentional, malicious, and unnecessary infliction of physical or mental suffering on a student

DARE. a program that addresses the dangers of drug abuse; Drug Awareness Resistance Education is usually presented by a police officer in conjunction with school personnel

defensive response. a self-protective approach in response to a serious event; in schools such a reaction may be made in the event of an attack on the building population, severe weather, or an internal threat

delayed start. a process whereby school has a postponed opening time, often necessitated by changing weather conditions or potential emergency situations

detention. an assigned consequence for fairly minor acts of misbehavior

dress code. an enforced rule regarding the appropriate attire to wear in school; many schools have policies that outline the acceptable limits permitted in student dress

drill. a practice of an emergency procedure to rehearse needed actions in the event of a real emergency; periodic fire drills have been conducted for years in schools as a rehearsal for behaviors necessary for escaping a fire

drop and cover. a technique used in the event of a potential explosion or dangerous situation where standing or sitting might expose one to increased harm; often this protective stance is recommended when encountering severe weather or the discharge of weapons

drug test. a medical test to ascertain the presence of illegal drugs in a urine sample

due process. the right to a fair and unbiased hearing; students are entitled to an informal or formal hearing in front of the school board before a determination is made regarding their innocence or guilt and consequences are administered

early dismissal. releasing students before the regular dismissal time, often necessitated by an unforeseen emergency

Edinboro. Pennsylvania town that was the site of one of the many school-related shootings resulting in the death of a teacher

effective teaching. presentation of material in a manner whereby the optimum opportunity is provided for learning

emancipation. court-approved permission for an individual eighteen years of age or older to reside independently from and be released from parental interference

employee screening. initial review of applications to eliminate or select candidates before interviews are scheduled

ES. emotional support; a classification of students with emotional difficulties

evacuation. the process by which a building is abandoned for safety reasons; in emergency situations schools sometimes must be vacated to avoid harm or injury to the students and staff members

expulsion. a process whereby a student is not permitted to attend school for an extended period of time; expulsion is normally a decision made by the school board in response to a student being found guilty of a serious violation of school policy

FAPE. free appropriate public education, provided at public expense from preschool to secondary, that meets state standards and conforms to IEPs

field trip. the visit of a class or part of a class to a site outside the immediate location of the school for educational purposes; usually the trip is related to the curriculum and is sponsored and supervised by district employees

504 plan. a written agreement between the parents and the school that outlines accommodations for the education of a temporarily disabled child

harassment. physical, verbal, or written persecution of an individual

heterogeneous. grouping students in a random manner to allow for a mixture of abilities within the same class

homework. assigned work to be completed outside of school

homogeneous. grouping students according to their ability level in a specific subject area

host site. a location away from the home site used for temporary housing during an emergency; usually schools have plans to use existing facilities to house students until transportation can be arranged

IDEA. Individuals with Disabilities Education Act; thirteen categories of disabilities within which special placement is possible

identified children. children that meet the criteria to receive special instruction as outlined in an individual education plan

IEP. individual education plan; a set of goals designed to meet the needs of an identified child in school

immorality. a course of conduct that offends the morals of the community and sets a bad example for students

inclusion. the education of an identified special needs child in a regular classroom setting whenever educationally appropriate

incompetency. an incapacity to teach arising out of a lack of substantive knowledge of the subject, a lack of ability, or a lack of desire to teach using proper methodology

in loco parentis. in place of the parent

in-service. training provided for staff members in a variety of areas; often entire days are devoted to workshops and training sessions on new programs, innovative techniques, and improvements in education

intemperance. a loss of self-control, including use of excessive force or excessive alcohol consumption

IST. instructional support team; often part of the screening for students experiencing difficulty at school

jargon. the terms and acronyms used in a profession; usually the educational "shorthand" used by educators when communicating about the learning process

kinetic learner. a student that learns best when exposed to participatory involvement in instruction

LEA. local educational agency; in cases related to special education it is normally the school (principal)

lecturing. technique of presenting instructional material verbally

lesson plan. an outline or plan for teaching a specific series of lessons for a specific segment of time

lockout/lockdown. a process used to secure a classroom or building in the event of a serious situation or emergency; often implemented as a protective stance when danger is suspected or encountered; when in effect, access to the building or classroom is denied to all unauthorized personnel

LRE. least restrictive environment; related to the placement of special needs children in regular classes whenever educationally practical

LS. learning support; a designation for children identified as having some special need related to their learning

mainstreaming. the forerunner of the term inclusion (see inclusion)

manifestation determination. determination of the relationship between misconduct and disability by considering an evaluation's diagnostic results, observation of the child, and the IEP in effect; if the misbehavior is not related to the disability school punishment may be imposed, pending parental appeal

MDT. multidisciplinary team; usually required to place a child in special education

memorandum of understanding. an agreement between the school system and local emergency responders outlining the protocols for dealing with emergencies within the school; normally police and fire departments meet and agree to the delineation of responsibilities and jurisdiction over emergency activities in the school

merit plan. a plan whereby teachers or administrators may receive compensation for successfully completing tasks or goals beyond the normal expectations of the district

negligence. the failure or refusal to do what one should be doing as an employee

No Child Left Behind. a federal law (January 2002) mandating accountability for student achievement, increased flexibility and local control, greater role for parents, and greater emphasis on scientifically based instruction

NORA. notice of recommended assignment

peer mediation. a process by which students that have a conflict can sit down and discuss alternatives to violence with the help of a mediator; most schools permit students to pursue this approach in an attempt to reduce violence and aggression within the schools

permanent certification. a license to continue teaching for a specific period of time up to ninety-nine years

permanent record. a student's record, parts of which remain with the school after graduation; normally the documentation of a student's educational record follows the student as he or she moves from school to school

principal. the educational leader of the individual school buildings; most often an educator that has had experience teaching and additional training in administration of school policies, curriculum, and management

probable cause. a requirement for police before a person or thing can be searched; in schools, having a strong reason to believe that a violation of school policy has taken place or a criminal act has occurred provides a valid reason to pursue a search

protocol. the preestablished steps in a procedure, as in following the approved steps in a crisis plan, the chain of command, or the procedures needed to meet a present need

PSSA. Pennsylvania State Student Assessment

PTA/PTO. Parent Teacher Association or Parent Teacher Organization

quality point average. the cumulative average of grades earned

rapport. establishing a good relationship with another, as in an open communications network with students

reasonable suspicion. a strong belief or suspicion that a violation of a policy or rule has occurred; in schools, principals need a reasonable suspicion to search a student or locker

REI. Regular Education Initiative

retention. the holding of a student for a second year at the same grade level

role-playing. the act of performing as another person for instructional purposes

safety. similar to security but including the internal and external day-to-day protection of children and staff from injury; usually involves attention to safety procedures in place, clear hallways, and inspection of facilities to guard against hazardous conditions

school board. a body of appointed or elected individuals that oversee the operation of the school district; also referred to as the board of school directors; normally the board investigates, discusses, and votes on proposed changes in the district's operating procedures, including the educational program

security. the safety of a school building against internal and external threats; safeguards against severe weather, violent attacks, localized industrial accidents, and community emergencies are included in a school's security procedures

SED. seriously emotionally disturbed

simulation. a drill conducted with attention to making the practice as real as possible; often the exercise is planned and executed as if the actual event is occurring

substitute teacher. a certified teacher temporarily employed to fill in for a regular teacher

superintendent. the educational leader of a school district; usually an experienced educator hired by the board of school directors to lead the district's educational program

suspension. a process whereby a student is not permitted to attend school for a short period of time; a suspension is normally assigned for periods of time from three to ten days as a result of a student's disregard for school rules

tabletop exercise. a rehearsal of an emergency situation with a small group of leaders; often schools conduct these exercises to evaluate the readiness of first responders in the building

tenure. a state guarantee of continued certification within certain parameters

tip line/hot line. method whereby individuals can anonymously contact the school to report potential danger

to go box. a container that contains items felt necessary in the event that the school must be evacuated during an emergency; contents may include school maps, medications, class lists, first aid kits, emergency phone numbers, and other items potentially needed at an evacuation center

unsatisfactory rating. the measurement of a teacher's inability to meet district expectations, failure to deliver appropriate instruction as judged by the district, or gross and persistent violation of school rules

weapon. any item that might cause harm to another person; schools classify many items as weapons, sometimes depending on how the items are used

zero tolerance. a policy that defines and outlines a severe consequence for violation of a school policy for which there will be no leniency; normally the possession of an illegal drug, weapon, or other item that could cause harm to others is included in such a policy

zigzag pattern. a technique recommended for use during an escape from a situation where a weapon might be discharged; police often recommend that students flee the dangerous situation by running from side to side in a zigzag fashion

Index

About the Author

Dr. Larry J. Stevens received his bachelor's degree in art education from Pennsylvania State University, two master's degrees from Edinboro University of Pennsylvania, and a doctorate in school administration from the State University of New York at Buffalo. In addition to teaching in public schools for thirteen years, he has served as a secondary and elementary principal for twenty-two years. Dr. Stevens has earned his Superintendent's Letter of Eligibility, certification as Supervisor of Curriculum and Instruction, and administrative certificates in both elementary and secondary administration. Recently retired from public school administration, he has taught graduate classes in school administration at Edinboro University of Pennsylvania and Gannon University and has served as a Safe Schools and crisis response consultant. He has presented numerous professional programs on various administrative topics both locally and nationally.

His published articles include "Administrative Techniques: The Principal's Time" (1984); "Administrative Planning Guide" (1985); "Instructional Leadership: A Single District Study of the Multiple Perceptions of Central Office Administrators, Principals, and Elementary Teachers" (1996); and "Development of a Critical Incident Plan" (1997). His published books include *An Administrative Handbook: A View from the Elementary Principal's Desk* (2001) and *A Critical Incident Planning and Development Guide: An Administrative Handbook* (2002).